# BOLD
## moves

# BOLD
## moves

CRAIG ETHEREDGE

Published by discipleFIRST.com

Published by discipleFIRST, 5405 Pleasant Run
Colleyville, TX 76034.

Unless otherwise noted, scripture quotations are from the ESV®
Bible (The Holy Bible, English Standard Version®), copyright © 2001
by Crossway, a publishing ministry of Good News Publishers. Used
by permission. All rights reserved.

Scripture quotations marked NLT are taken from the Holy Bible, New
Living Translation, copyright © 1996. Used by permission of Tyndale
House Publishers, Inc., Wheaton, Illinois 60189. All rights reserved.

Scripture quotations marked (NLT) are taken from the Holy Bible, New
Living Translation, copyright ©1996, 2004, 2007, 2013 by Tyndale
House Foundation. Used by permission of Tyndale House Publishers,
Inc., Carol Stream, Illinois 60188. All rights reserved.

ISBN: 978-1-586-95490-1

Library of Congress Control Number:  2016901386

PRINTED IN THE UNITED STATES OF AMERICA

Book Design and Layout: Russell Lake - SeedStudios.com

First Edition, Second Printing

"This is a must read for anyone serious about helping their church transition to be more effective at making disciples. This book is simple and practical while being Jesus-focused and local church centered. It will encourage very practical ways for you and your church to become better at making disciples. And most important, this book is written by a senior pastor who has transitioned several ministries toward disciple making, and is now helping multitudes of other churches to do the same. These seven bold moves have captured the essence of what is needed for the American church."

– Dr. Dann Spader, author of *4 Chair Discipling* and *Walking As Jesus Walked*, Founder of Sonlife Ministries and President of Global Youth Initiative.

"Courage is knowing that you are risking reputation, money, or even your life and then doing the right thing regardless of cost. Craig Etheredge's *Bold Moves* is an act of courage. Not only because he is calling out his fellow pastors, but because he has called himself out as well. He must live it, and show his commitment to it. Like his golfing buddy said, 'Craig, you just need to define success and commit yourself to those results.' There are not many willing to cast aside the 'success' of current popular church culture and dig in and make disciples. Craig has demonstrated that he is one and if you want to join him, then read this book."

– Bill Hull, author of *Conversion & Discipleship,
Jesus Christ Disciple Maker, The Disciple
Making Pastor,* and *The Disciple Making Church.*
Leader of The Bonhoeffer Project.

"Pastor Craig Etheredge is not just musing about disciple making, he has been living it, and guiding First Baptist Colleyville through the arduous journey of becoming a disciple-making church. *Bold Moves* captures the struggle of leading a local church to place disciple making at the core of its DNA and culture. Craig does not cut corners, but lays out time-tested Biblical principles for raising up spiritual generations of disciples in the context of the local church. Any pastor or church leader serious about disciple making will find this book invaluable in leading individuals and congregations to become disciple makers."

– Eddie Broussard,
Vice-President, International Executive Team
The Navigators

# DEDICATION

To the men who invested in my life and who constantly challenge me to make disciples who make disciples... thank you.

Ron Etheredge, David Guinn, John Repass,
Jerry Fine, Herman Reece, Bill Hull, Dann Spader
and Eddie Broussard

To the staff and leadership of First Colleyville for their deep passion to ignite a movement of multiplication in our lifetime.

To the Southern Baptists of Texas Convention for their partnership and unwavering support of disciple making in the local church.

# TABLE OF CONTENTS

"**Prove** to
the world that
**you** are
**My disciples**."
– Jesus

# INTRODUCTION

Bold moves matter.

They matter so much that nothing of great significance ever gets done without someone making a bold move. Think about it. There would be no July 4th without the bold moves of a few men tossing tea in the harbor. There would be no civil rights movement without the bold move of Rosa Parks staying in her seat. There would be no rock 'n' roll without the bold moves of Elvis or the Beatles. There would be no space travel without the bold move of Neil Armstrong's "one small step for man" on the face of the moon. Bold moves shake up the status quo.

## SUMMER OF '84

One of my first bold moves took place during the summer of 1984. I had just graduated from high school in the panhandle of Texas, and my future was stretching out in front of me. I couldn't wait to get out of my small town. I was ready for something new. But I wasn't excited about leaving a certain girl behind. I first met Liz in the fifth grade. My dad was a worship leader and had taken a new position at the church in town, so we packed up and moved from central Texas out to the wind-blowing, sandy skies of West Texas. It was like moving to another planet. It actually rains mud there. I can remember seeing storms blow the dirt up in the sky, and as the rain fell it mixed with the dirt to make mud pellets as it hit the car windshield. Got to love it. My first week in the new town, I noticed some kids bouncing on a trampoline next door. As I peeked through the wooden slats of the fence I saw a cute dark-headed girl bobbing up and down. I thought to myself, "Hey, she's pretty cute," but it would take me almost eight years to get her attention. During that time we became close friends. We went to each other's birthday parties. We had class together. I played football. She was a cheerleader. But on that summer night after graduation, I decided to take Liz out on an evening drive. It wasn't uncommon for us to just hang out and talk. We had been friends for as long as we both could remember, but this night was different. As we sat in the car talking about the changes ahead of us, Liz started to cry. I put my arm around her to comfort her (as a good friend would!) And then it happened. She looked up right at the moment I looked down, and suddenly we were nose to nose. Now freeze for a minute. It's weird how thoughts can run through your mind in a split second. I remember thinking, "Now's the time to kiss her. You will never get this chance again. You snooze, you lose!" The other thought was, "Don't ruin a good friendship…things are changing anyway. Back off!" So what happened? That night I took a bold move. I kissed Liz. Now, twenty-eight years of marriage and two daughters later, it has been the boldest and best move of my life!

Bold moves are necessary if you want to accomplish anything in life, either personal or professional. The passive route just never gets anything done. Any new or bold innovation starts with someone taking a chance, assuming the risk, defying the odds, and making a move.

Bold moves redefine boundaries.

Bold moves stir up controversy.

Bold moves draw critics and followers.

Bold moves initiate movements.

Bold moves change the world.

## JESUS' BOLD MOVE

Anytime God wants to initiate something new, he calls one of his own to make a bold move. You can count on it.

It was certainly bold for Abraham to leave his retirement plans in Ur and venture out into an uncharted land. It was bold for David to face off against the giant, Goliath. It was bold for Moses to return to Egypt where he was a wanted man. It was bold for Joshua to circle Jericho. It was bold for Elijah to build an altar. It was bold for Daniel to pray. It was bold for Nehemiah to initiate a building project. God always begins his new work by calling his people to make extraordinary, risk-taking, hair-raising, wisdom-defying bold moves. Without them, nothing great ever happens.

The greatest bold moves of all were reserved for Jesus. If I were to ask you, "What were Jesus' bold moves?" you would probably say something like: leaving heaven, confronting the Pharisees, enduring the cross, maybe even the resurrection—you can't get bolder than that! Did you know, though, that there were a series of bold moves Jesus made early in his ministry that were so critical, so strategic that if he had not taken them, the movement would have died before it had a chance to live?

John the Baptist was wildly popular. Massive crowds came from all over Israel and bordering countries to hear his hard-hitting prophetic message of repentance. John was like the Billy Graham of his day. He was a magnet to the people and a lightening rod to the religious leaders. Whether you agreed with John or not, there was no denying the fact that excitement was stirring and the people could sense it. Eighteen months earlier, John had baptized Jesus in the Jordan River, just north of the Dead Sea. At that time he started pointing people to Jesus, declaring, *"Behold, the Lamb of God who takes away the sin of the world!"* (John 1.29). Some followed Jesus, but the crowds were still gravitating to John. Then tragedy struck. John was put in prison by Herod Antipas, the Governor of the Galilee region, for publicly exposing Herod Antipas' illicit affair with his own brother's wife, Herodius. With John out of the picture, the crowds were left without a leader and the movement could have begun to dissipate. But in that moment, Jesus made a series of bold moves.

> When He heard that John had been arrested, He withdrew into Galilee. He left Nazareth behind and went to live in Capernaum by the sea, in the region of Zebulun and Naphtali. This was to fulfill what was spoken through the prophet Isaiah: Land of Zebulun and land of Naphtali, along the sea road, beyond the Jordan, Galilee of the Gentiles! The people who live in darkness have seen a great light, and for those living in the shadowland of death, light has dawned. From then on Jesus began to preach, "Repent, because the kingdom of heaven has come near!" As He was walking along the Sea of Galilee, He saw two brothers, Simon, who was called Peter, and his brother Andrew. They were casting a net into the sea, since they were fishermen. "Follow Me," He told them, "and I will make you fish for people!" Matthew 4.12-19

Jesus stepped into the vacuum of leadership and made four bold moves. First, he moved his home base of operation from Nazareth (his hometown) to Capernaum. Capernaum was a thriving city on the north shore of the

Sea of Galilee. It would have been the equivalent of moving from a small West Texas town to the big city of Dallas. Second, Jesus began to preach the message that John the Baptist had been preaching, namely "Repent for the kingdom of heaven has come." Third, Jesus began to give leadership to the movement. From this point forward, John would never again be the focal point. His work was done. Now all eyes were on Jesus. Finally, Jesus started calling out men to form his leadership team. He had been grooming Peter and Andrew, James and John for this moment. Now it was their time to make a bold move of their own. As a result of Jesus' moves, the ministry continued to grow and the movement of God went to a whole new level. From this point forward miracles exploded, Jesus' popularity soared, and leaders multiplied. If Jesus hadn't made these moves, my guess is the movement would have smoldered, fizzled, and slowly died out. Let me draw out a principle here that is vitally important. For ministry to move forward, it requires leaders to make Spirit-directed, risk-defying, faith-emboldened bold moves. These moves create momentum, increase focus, infuse energy, establish new norms, surface new leaders, and result in growth. You are simply not going to get where you want to go apart from making some bold moves. If there was ever a time when the church needed leaders to make bold moves, that time is now.

# THE SMOLDERING MOVEMENT

It doesn't take much to see that the church in North America is struggling. What is a raging fire in the East is down to a flicker in the West. The church is in serious trouble. The facts speak for themselves.[1]

» Every year, more than 4,000 churches close their doors, compared to just over 1,000 new church starts!

» Every year, 2.7 million church members fall into inactivity.

» From 1990 to 2000, the combined membership of all Protestant denominations in the United States declined by almost 5 million members (9.5 percent), while the U.S. population increased by 24 million (11 percent).

» The United States now ranks third (3rd), after China and India, in the number of people who are not professing Christians. In other words, the U.S. is becoming an ever-increasing "unreached people group."

» Half of all churches in the U.S. have not added any new members to their ranks in the last two years.

These facts are sobering, even breathtaking. What is happening to the church in North America? Some people are quick to blame a growing secular culture that isn't interested in the gospel. Some blame the church for

---

[1]     www.churchleadership.org

using antiquated techniques and not staying "culturally relevant." Others blame immigration and the infusion of new religious ideologies. I don't blame any of those things. The problem isn't the culture. The early church flourished in a dark and hostile environment, and even today the fastest growing churches are in areas of great persecution and resistance. The problem isn't techniques. No style of music or slick marketing strategy can bring about life change. The problem isn't competing ideologies. The gospel is the gospel for all nations, tribes, and cultures. So, what is the problem? The problem is that the church has forgotten its intended purpose, to make disciples of Jesus Christ who will turn around and make more disciples.

## WAKE UP CALL

I'll never forget sitting behind my desk staring at the report in front of me. It was my first time to be a lead pastor. I had come to this church from a growing suburban church in Texas that had plenty of leaders and resources, and now I was leading an inner-city church in Oklahoma City facing all kinds of challenges. The church had been static for almost a decade with little growth. All the while, the neighborhoods around the church had slowly begun to change, becoming more ethnically and socio-economically diverse. Before long, it became obvious that the people in the pews on Sundays didn't look like the people in the community around the church Monday through Saturday. At first no one really noticed the changes. The church seemed resilient, impervious to the changing climate. But over time, the cracks began to surface. Families were choosing to move out of the neighborhood and into the suburbs for better schools. Once that happened, it was just a matter of time before they would leave the church to find one closer to where they lived. I could almost set my watch and predict when certain families would leave. By the time their kids moved into middle school, they were all but gone. Every family that left felt like a knife in my heart. There was a slow leak, a constant drain of people quietly leaving the church. On the other hand, because the people in our church were different than the community, it became increasingly hard to get people in the community to come into the church. They saw the church as a "rich, white, and professional church," not a place where they would fit in. No matter how hard we tried to change that perception, people in the neighborhood never seemed to stick. Our members who lived in the suburbs and had decided to stay were faithful and devoted to the ministry, but they could never seem to get their neighbors and friends to come to church with them. No one wanted to go into "that part of town" to go to church. You can see the problem. With people quietly leaving for the suburbs, and both the people in the community and the suburbs unwilling to come, the church was on a slow fade. No program was going to fix this problem. It wasn't a matter of music style. It wasn't an issue of better preaching. It wasn't even an issue of facilities. Many people would say, "Craig, it's not you or the church. We love it here. But we just have to make this move for our kids." As a young pastor, it seemed to be an unfixable problem. A knot I couldn't unravel. I spent many sleepless nights praying for God to give me direction. I didn't relocate my family to a new state and choose to lead this church only to watch it dwindle on my watch. So the decision was made to hire a consultant. After an extensive survey of our people and what seemed like hundreds of hours of intense meetings, his report was sitting on my desk. I took a deep breath, and turned the first page. In one sense I was expecting the worst— some kind of final verdict that would say all hope was lost. On the other hand, I had a sense of hope that maybe, just maybe, this guy was going to see something I had missed and would give me some quick and easy steps out of this situation. His conclusion was that the church had a severe case of "ethnicitus"—a cultural and ethnic dissimilarity between those in the church and those in the community. I knew that already. What I didn't know was how to fix it. The next words were like a punch in the gut. *Ethnicitus is terminal.* In his opinion, the church was swimming upstream against the current of social change and it was only a matter of time before it slowly tired out and quit. Only a total relocation could save the church. We had already considered a relocation option, but it wasn't feasible. If you plotted our church membership on a map, it would look like a shotgun pattern with the church in the middle. Our membership was perfectly positioned around the church. A move in any direction would be moving away from three-quarters of our people.

To add to that, a church in our area had recently relocated and it was a disaster. The church eventually split over the decision and ended up weaker than it was in the first place. The people in our church weren't open to relocation. Closing the report, I buried my face in my hands. What was I going to do? For the next few weeks, I cleared the calendar to spend time praying, fasting, and seeking God. I spent time alone. I gathered our staff for early morning prayer meetings. From that time of soul-searching and yearning, I discovered something. I was looking for a silver bullet that would fix my problems. I wanted a quick fix, a program in a box, something to stop the bleeding and get us back on track to being a mega church. But I discovered that our real problem was that we had forgotten why we were in the community in the first place. We had lost our passion for evangelism. We were not living in true community. We were not investing in people spiritually and seeing lives changed. We weren't making disciples of Jesus who could, in turn, make more disciples. Out of that moment of crisis, I realized that before the church could change, I had to change. I had to stop trying to pull new gimmicks out of my ministerial bag of tricks. I had to stop running to conferences and different churches, seeking out different models of how to do the ministry. I had to learn what it meant to be a disciple of Jesus Christ and how to make disciples. Unfortunately, that was something I never saw in church growing up and something I never learned how to do in seminary. Over the next few years, I led that church through seven bold moves. Not every move was met with a standing ovation. Some were hard. Remember, bold moves often attract followers and critics. There were times of exhilarating, heart-pumping victory, as well as devastating disappointments. Along the way I also saw God do amazing work in that church, so much that it completely transformed the community and the whole city took notice and applauded. Along the way, I also saw God do amazing work in me. He lit a passion in me to make disciples and invest my life in a few who could change the world.

Let me warn you before you read any further. This book is not a quick fix. I'm not going to give you oversimplified answers to your complicated challenges. What I'm laying out in these pages will not be easy. It will require of you the highest level of leadership and grit and determination and faith. Recently, I was sitting with a young worship ministry leader at a coffee shop not far from my house. He was six months into his first ministry position, but he had already noticed that the senior pastor was passive and indecisive. When he asked the pastor about it, the pastor replied, "I just don't want to upset anyone." Let me be clear. Leaders will always upset someone. Fear of unhappy people only paralyzes a leader and makes him ineffective. What is required of leaders is godly wisdom and courage. Wisdom to know what to do, and courage to take a deep breath and do it.

I have a favorite coffee cup that was given to me by a young pastor whom I discipled many years ago. It has a picture of John Wayne on the front. On the inside, at a place where only the drinker can see, it says, "Courage is being scared to death—but saddling up anyway." Are you ready to saddle up? Are you ready to make some bold moves that will position your church for eternal impact? If your answer is yes, then keep reading. In the pages to follow, I will unpack seven bold moves your church will need to navigate to become a healthy, multiplying, disciple-making church. And here is my promise to you. If you set your heart and mind on making these bold moves, God will be with you. He will lead you and He will bless you because you will be doing ministry the way Jesus did it. So, let's get started.

What I'm laying out in these pages **will not be easy**. It will require of you the **highest level** of **grit** and **determination** and **faith**.

# SEVEN BOLD MOVES TO BECOMING A DISCIPLE-MAKING CHURCH

**Fear** of unhappy people only **paralyzes** a leader and makes him ineffective. What is **required** of leaders is **godly wisdom** and **courage**. Wisdom to know what to do, and **courage** to take a deep breath and **do it**.

# MOVE FROM CHURCH MODELS TO CHRIST'S MODEL

Church leaders love models.

Pastors seem to be naturally drawn to the latest and greatest trends in ministry. Over the past twenty years, I've seen models come and go. I can remember when "Flake's formula" was the rage for growing Sunday Schools in Baptist churches. Arthur Flake was a department store salesman from Winona, Mississippi, who began to volunteer in his local church and developed a strategy for growing groups. Although he never attended seminary or pastored a church, Flake became the first Director for Sunday School for Southern Baptists in 1920, and his five-point formula influenced churches all across North

America and the Pacific. This was the model I was taught in seminary. After Flake came bus ministry. Walter Stuart Beebe was running a gas station in southern Florida when a young lady gave him a Gospel tract. He later came to faith in Christ and became a pastor. But he was best known as "Mr. Bus" because he began the bus ministry movement in the early 70s that spread like wildfire across the country. Churches would rent or buy a fleet of buses and bring kids to church. Beebe directed some of the largest bus ministries in the nation from Florida to Indiana, including Jerry Falwell's church in Lynchburg, Virginia. In the 1980s came the "attractional model" that focused on seeker-sensitive worship experiences designed to attract the unchurched. Willow Creek and Saddleback were the trail blazers of that movement. In the early 90s, the Pentecostal minister, Carl George popularized the "meta church model," emphasizing not large gatherings, but intimate, small home groups he called cells. By the late 1990s to the early 2000s a new trend was developing called "missional communities." This model originated with St. Thomas' Crookes Church in Sheffield, England and proposed that churches should not concentrate on large attractive worship services or small home groups, but should instead serve the needs of the community. Early adapters promoted "random acts of kindness" and "social justice" as a means to evangelism and church growth. In early 2000, bloggers Frank Viola and Neil Cole promoted the "organic church model," defining church as a rapidly reproducing gathering of three to twenty people with little structure or organizational leadership. In the last ten years, the "multi-site model" has become increasingly popular. It was pioneered by Larry Osborne, Greg Ferguson, and Craig Groeschel. In 1990 there were only ten multi-site churches in America, but by 2012 there were over five thousand churches using this model. The fastest growing churches in America are using a multi-site strategy. Today, a whole new language circulates on church blogs and conferences using terms like "radical," "relational," "tribal," "fundamental," "emergent," "reformed," "egalitarian," "complementarian," "cessationist," "charismatic," and on it goes. I'm sitting here with a book on my desk that urges pastors to "identify their tribe" and find their model. When I get around certain groups of pastors, they are quick to show their tribal label and they want to see mine. Church conferences are all about promoting the latest models and tribes. Mega church pastors take the stage like rock stars and talk about how many thousands of people attend their services and how many followers they have on Twitter. All the while, the pastor in the seat, slugging it out in a struggling church, has two options: either he can leave discouraged ("I'll never be as successful or as cool as he is. I guess I'm a failure.") or leave envious ("I want what he's got. I want to be just like him. I'll mimic him so maybe I can be successful, too.") Either option is bad. In the meantime, the church at large is shrinking. Now don't get me wrong. I'm not saying that church models or tribal distinctives are bad. In fact, each of the models I've mentioned has been used by God to advance the church and to reach people. I'm thankful for each of them. Additionally, throughout history the church has always adapted and morphed into various shapes and models—sometimes for the better, sometimes for the worse. The church has always been tribal, dividing and gathering along the lines of theology and practice. That's not my concern. My concern is that somewhere in all the current dialogue about models, tribes, and trends, the model of Jesus is getting lost.

## THE FORGOTTEN MODEL

Now the minute I say that, I'm going to get a reaction. I can already see you scribbling your objections in the margin of this book. The truth is, every model claims it is Jesus' model for ministry. The attractional people point to how Jesus drew large crowds with his relevant teaching. The organic people point to Jesus' small group of twelve. The missional people point to Jesus' healing ministry and compassion for the poor. The social justice people point to Jesus' defense of those who couldn't defend themselves. The radical people point to Jesus' call to sacrifice and self-denial. Everybody claims Jesus as the poster child for their ministry model. But I am convinced that there is a bigger picture which is often missed. As a young pastor, I have to confess I had never really studied the life of Jesus looking for his model of ministry. I had studied the teachings of Jesus in depth. I had studied the ministry of Jesus and sought to emulate it to some degree. I had studied the person of Jesus and certainly preached what he did for us on the cross. But I had never looked at Jesus as a model for ministry. I had never looked at Jesus' ministry chronologically to discover what he did in year one, year two, and year three. When I began to do that, the lights started coming on. I began to see Jesus and his ministry in a whole new way that was life-changing.

I am convinced that Jesus, Himself, is the model for ministry. Throughout scripture, we are told to walk as he walked (I John 2.6), do what he did (John 14.12), and think as he thought (Philippians 2.5). Jesus' main invitation was "follow me." In Greek, *akoloutheo* means *"to follow"* or *"to go behind"* someone in a physical and at times in an *"intellectual, moral, and religious sense."* The idea is that one holds steadfastly to and is being conformed to the example of another.[2] When my girls were younger, we would go to the beach on vacation. Imagine me and my wife walking along the beach at sunset, and with every step we leave a trail of footprints in the sand behind us. Now imagine one of my daughters following behind me, putting her foot in my footprint. She's walking in the steps of her dad. That's the idea here. To follow Jesus means to walk in his steps. It means to follow his example, to imitate his life, his heart, his character, and his behavior. The whole purpose of Jesus' three plus years of ministry was to raise up men who were just like him and who could do ministry the way Jesus taught them to do it. And he was successful. When the apostles stood boldly facing off the religious leaders in

---

2    *Theological Dictionary of the New Testament.*

4.13, the skeptics were shocked and took note that these men had been with Jesus. I love this verse because I can just see the religious leaders taking a sidebar and whispering amongst themselves, "These guys talk just like Jesus, they act just like Jesus, and they've got the same swag as Jesus!" That's what Jesus wanted then, and it is what he wants today – men and women who look and act like him. The Apostle Paul understood this. He said to the Corinthian Church, *"Imitate me as I imitate Christ"* (I Corinthians 11.1). The writer of Hebrews challenged new believers. *"Let us fix our eyes on Jesus, the author and perfecter of our faith..."* (Hebrews 12.2, NIV). Again he says, *"Fix your thoughts on Jesus"* (Hebrews 3.1, NIV). Obviously, Jesus was intended to be our focus. In order to do that, you have to take a serious and hard look at the life and ministry of Jesus. Not just at its parts, but at the whole. As a young pastor of a struggling inner-city church, I realized that during all my church experience and seminary training, I had never really taken a serious look at how Jesus did ministry. I saw bits and fragments, like scattered pieces of a jigsaw puzzle, but I had never put those pieces together and seen the comprehensive picture of what Jesus did, how he did it, when he did it, and why he did it. That's where I started, and that's where you will need to start. In this book I will give you a glimpse into Jesus' ministry model. Along the way, I will suggest some ways you can implement that model in the life of your church. Years after embarking upon this journey, I'm convinced that Jesus' model is the only model that is successful over the long haul and is the only model that produces genuine, reproducing disciples and healthy churches.

## MISCONCEPTIONS ABOUT JESUS' MINISTRY MODEL

It is hard to believe, but not everyone is excited about using Jesus as the model for ministry. It truly baffles me that we look to Jesus for our salvation, we look to Jesus as an example in godly living, we look to Jesus as a source of wisdom in teaching, but we don't look to Jesus as model for ministry. Some pastors I've talked to have been outright resistant to the thought. They are insulted by the idea. As I've listened to their complaints, I have heard some consistent misconceptions about Jesus' ministry that need to be tackled head on. Chances are good that you have some of these misconceptions right now.

**Misconception #1—Jesus didn't have a strategic ministry plan.**

Many pastors don't think that Jesus had an intentional plan of ministry. As they read the gospels, it looks like Jesus randomly flowed from one village to the next, performing miracles and teaching without any strategic forethought. The gospels have become a resource for the teaching of Jesus and the life of Jesus, but not the ministry of Jesus. Honestly, that was where I found myself in my early days of ministry. I looked more to the epistles for instruction on ministry and the church, not to Jesus. To be honest, I never really spent much time digging into the life of Christ. Then I was exposed to a small book by Robert Coleman, oddly titled, *The Master Plan of Evangelism*. I say it's oddly titled because at first glimpse you would think it is a book about how to share your faith. Actually, it's a look at the ministry of Jesus. In his book, Coleman points out that Jesus had an intentional plan, and he worked that plan to perfection. I remember reading this book for the first time. I had just graduated with my Master's Degree from Seminary, and once I started reading, I couldn't put it down. It was a game changer for me. I had never read anything like it before. Listen to Coleman describe Jesus' intentional strategy.

"His (Jesus') life was ordered by his objective. Everything he did and said was part of the whole pattern. It had significance because it contributed to the ultimate purpose of his life in redeeming the world for God. This was the motivating vision governing his behavior. His steps were ordered by it. Mark it well. Not for one moment did Jesus lose sight of this goal. That is why it is so important to observe the way Jesus maneuvered to achieve his objective. The Master disclosed God's strategy for world conquest...It is tremendously revealing to study it. Serious reflection at this point will bring the student of Christ to some profound and perhaps shattering conclusions, though the realization will likely be slow and arduous. In fact, at first glance it might even appear that Jesus had no plan. Another approach might discover some particular technique but miss the underlying patter of it all. This is one of the marvels of his strategy. It is so unassuming and silent that it is unnoticed by the hurried churchman. But when the realization of his controlling method finally dawns on the open mind of the disciple he will be amazed at its simplicity and wonder how he could have ever failed to see it before. Nevertheless, when his plan is reflected on, the basic philosophy is so different from that of the modern church that its implications are nothing less than revolutionary."[3]

Not too long after reading Coleman's book, I met a pastor named Bill Hull. I was taking doctoral classes at the Trinity Evangelical Divinity School (TEDS) in Chicago and Bill was teaching a seminar. I was fascinated with the concept that Jesus had an actual plan. We met for dinner after class at a small restaurant in town and talked about Jesus and local church ministry. I felt like Bill knew exactly what I was experiencing because he had been a pastor as well. When I got back to Oklahoma I read Bill's first book. The old version had a royal blue cover simply titled, *Jesus Christ Disciple Maker*. Not that sexy a title, but it communicated. In the book, Bill described the four stages Jesus led his men through to produce disciples and disciple makers. I remember reading the following statement. It's still underlined and highlighted; the

---

3    *Master Plan of Evangelism*, page 24.

page is dog-eared in my copy. *"A leader should usually choose the option that will, in the long run, reach the most people with the message of eternal life. This is why discipleship is ordained by God: because its design is to multiply through people the good news to the entire world. This is the essence of the Great Commission."*[4] God was opening my mind to the idea that Jesus had a plan and I needed to understand it and work it. Not long after that I bought a copy of *A Harmony of the Gospels*, by Dr. Robert L. Thomas and Dr. Stanley N. Gundry. If you are not familiar with a harmony of the gospels, it places all the texts of the gospels into chronological order. In it you can see what Jesus did first, second, third, and so on. I still pore over that book today, now stained with ink markings, penciled notes, highlights, and turned down pages. It's even frayed on the spine where one of my dogs decided to use it for a chew toy. By the time I was nearing the end of my doctoral work, I chose to write my dissertation on how Jesus used small groups to raise up and train leaders. I was beginning to see Jesus in a whole new light. No longer was I blindly grasping at one facet of Jesus' ministry. I was beginning to see a chronological order, an intentional process, and a strategic plan Jesus had for making disciples. Once my project was complete and I was ready to defend my dissertation, I came into contact with Dr. Dann Spader. Dann was teaching large conferences all across the country about the life of Christ and Jesus' plan for disciple making. Like everything else,

---

4    *Jesus Christ Disciples Maker*, Hull, page 81.

I scarfed up his books and manuals. Interestingly, though the terminology was different, Spader was saying the same things that Coleman and Hull were saying—Jesus had a clear plan for making disciples. On September 12, 2001, the day after the towers fell in New York City, Dann sat on the evaluation team as I defended my doctoral project on disciple making. As I returned to Oklahoma City, I had a new sense of excitement. I was determined to put Jesus' plan into practice no matter what. I called staff meetings to study Jesus' plan and sat through hours of training. I can remember banging out definitions, processes, and details (we will get to all of that later in the book). I was compelled to do ministry Jesus' way. I still am.

Just a few weeks ago I sat down in a restaurant with two young professionals. One of them, Rick, attends our church; the other doesn't. At the time, Rick had been coming for a few years, staying mostly on the fringe because of his fast-paced life and high-pressure career. I took him out for coffee and challenged him to take the next step in following Jesus. He agreed to meet me one night in my office. When he showed up there were four other young business execs sitting around my conference table. For the next hour I talked to them about Jesus' plan for ministry. I drew it out on a piece a paper. I offered to invest in them for a period of time and train them to walk with Jesus in a deep, personal, and intimate way. They were all in. Over the next several weeks we met, prayed, studied, and encouraged. One night I challenged these racehorses to step it up a notch and recruit someone they could train. The wheels started turning. Several days later Rick asked me to join him for breakfast and he introduced me to another business friend. Rick had led his friend to Christ about a year earlier, but he never knew how to help him grow. As we sat at the table, I pulled out a napkin and drew out Jesus' plan for building world changers. The young executive watched my every pen stroke on the edge of his seat. When I finished, he said, with tears welling up in his eyes, "This is what I've been looking for. I'm all in!" Jesus had a plan, and his plan is compelling. His plan is what men and women need today, and they are begging for someone to show it to them. Our job, and our joy, is to do just that.

**Misconception #2—Jesus was God in the flesh; I'm not.**

Another objection to following Jesus' model goes like this: "Okay, Jesus may have had a plan, but he's JESUS...I'm not. There is no way I can do what Jesus did." Underneath that objection is a faulty Christology. Most pastors embrace the truth that Jesus is fully God. Colossians 1.15-17 states it clearly. *"He (Jesus) is the image of the invisible God, the firstborn of all creation. For by him all things were created, in heaven and on earth, visible and invisible, whether thrones or dominions or rulers or authorities—all things were created through him and for him."* (see also John 1.1,14; Hebrews 1.3; Colossians 1.19) Repeatedly, Jesus claimed to be God in the flesh. At one point Jesus said plainly, *"You are from below, I am from above. You are from this world, I am not of this world" (John 8.23).* It doesn't get much clearer than that. On another occasion Jesus said, *"My sheep hear my voice and I know them, and they follow me. I give them eternal life and they shall never perish, and no one will snatch them out of my hand. My Father, who has given them to me, is greater than all, and no one is able to snatch them out of my Father's hand. I and the Father are one."* With that, the religious leaders reached to pick up rocks to stone Jesus. When he asked why they were about kill him, they replied, *"Because you, being a man, make yourself God"* (John 10.27-30,33; see also John 5.17-18). Most pastors have no problem embracing Jesus as fully God. However, the scriptures also make it clear that Jesus was fully man. Jesus' favorite title for himself was "Son of Man." It is found eighty-one times in the New Testament gospels, and thirty of those are in the book of Matthew alone. It was a declaration of his humanity. Jesus wasn't a mystical person or a legend. He wasn't an illusion that only appeared to be human. He wasn't super-human, he was fully human. Hebrews 2.17 says that Jesus was like us "in every respect." He grew and developed just like us (Luke 2.52). He was tired and thirsty just like us (John 4.6-7). He grieved and he wept just like us (John 11.33-35). He was tempted just like us (Matthew 4.1-2). He suffered and died just like us (John 19.28-30). John, one of Jesus' closest friends and a part of Jesus' inner circle, said this about Jesus: *"We proclaim to you the one who existed from the beginning, whom we have heard and seen. We saw him with our own eyes and touched him with our own hands. He is the Word of life" (I John 1.1, NLT).* John was saying, "We know Jesus. He's not from this world. He is God. He existed before anything was made. But he is also fully human—we heard Jesus, we saw him with our own eyes, we touched him with our hands!" Jesus was fully human, in every way like us, with one exception; Jesus was without sin (Hebrews 4.15).

You may be asking, "What relevance does this have to leading my church and making disciples?" It has everything to do with it. Follow my thinking here. Let's press this thought a bit deeper. How could Jesus be both fully God and fully man at the same time? The answer is found in Philippians chapter two. The apostle Paul is speaking here about the nature of Jesus.

"...who, though he was in the form (morphe) of God, did not count equality with God a thing to be grasped, but emptied himself, by taking the form (morphe) of a servant, being born in the likeness of men." Philippians 2.6-7

Notice the word translated as "form" is the Greek word *morphe,* meaning "nature, substance." It's the same word from which we get metamorphosis, meaning to change forms. The word is used in two key instances in the following verses. Jesus pre-existed in the form (nature or substance) of God. He enjoyed equality with the Father. This is what Jesus was referring to in his high and priestly prayer when he prayed, *"And now, Father, glorify me in your own presence with the glory that I had with you before the world existed"* (John 17.5). But when Jesus came to earth, he became fully human. He took on the form (nature, substance) of a servant, *"being born in the likeness of men."* At the birth of Jesus, something miraculous happened. The Immortal God became Immanuel, "God with us" (Matthew 1.23). Eternity stepped into time. Deity took on humanity. Jesus stepped out of heaven and stepped into our world. This is the miracle of Christmas—the miracle of the incarnation. This came at a very high price. It required that Jesus "empty himself." The word Paul uses here is *kenoo*, which means to empty oneself or make oneself nothing. In the incarnation, Jesus did not cease being God. Rather, he temporarily veiled his heavenly glory so he could express his earthly humanity. He gave up his independent authority, choosing instead to humble himself, subjecting everything to the Father and relying completely upon the power of the Spirit. He set aside his personal riches in heaven and embraced the poverty of this world so we could become spiritually rich in him (2 Corinthians 8.9; Ephesians 1.3).

I love the show Undercover Boss. In every episode, a CEO of a major corporation disguises himself, then secretly enters at the bottom of the organization. No one really knows who he is. I remember one episode in which the CEO of a large fast food chain came disguised as a new trainee. He had to learn to mop the floors, wash the dishes, clean the food, and scrub the toilets. Along the way, the CEO was getting an idea of what was really going on inside the organization and what changes needed to be made. At no time did the CEO ever reveal his true identity. He couldn't call in any favors. He couldn't pull any strings. He couldn't leverage his CEO status in any way. He had to learn to do the job his employees were doing with the same resources they had. In a similar way, Jesus is the ultimate CEO over all creation. He came to earth in a way no one expected. Clothed in humanity. Born in poverty. Lived in obscurity. But he learned obedience. He trusted his Father. He depended on the Spirit. He studied and obeyed the scriptures. He lived in community. In using those resources, he ignited a movement and then told his followers to do the same. He told us to follow his example (I Peter 2.21), to live as he lived, walk as he walked, trust as he trusted, pray as he prayed, be courageous as he was courageous, rely on the Spirit as he relied on the Spirit, sacrifice as he sacrificed, and love as he loved. Jesus has provided all that you need in order to follow in his steps and make disciples who will change the world. As we walk together through these seven steps, I will show you how you can do just that!

**Misconception #3—The church age didn't start until after Jesus' resurrection.**

Some may suggest that Jesus couldn't be the model for ministry because the church age didn't begin until after Jesus' resurrection on the day of Pentecost. Therefore, the work Jesus did with the disciples predates the church and cannot be considered a model for ministry in the church. I disagree. In Matthew 16.18, Jesus states, "And I tell you, you are Peter, and on this rock I will build my church, and the gates of hell shall not prevail against it" (Matthew 16.18). The phrase, "build my church" is exactly what Jesus was doing during this earthly ministry. He was, in a very real and practical way, laying the foundation of the church with himself as the cornerstone and the men he trained as the foundation. The Apostle Paul acknowledged this when he wrote, "So then you are no longer strangers and aliens, but you are fellow citizens with the saints and members of the household of God, built on the foundation of the apostles and prophets, Christ Jesus himself being the cornerstone, in whom the whole structure, being joined together, grows into a holy temple in the Lord. In him you also are being built together into a dwelling place for God by the Spirit" (Ephesians 2.19-22). Years ago when Liz and I first moved to Oklahoma City, we built our first house. I can still remember the foundation being poured. We walked among the studs and prayed over each room as it was being built. We wrote scriptures on the foundation slab. Finally, the project was complete and we celebrated on move-in day. If someone were to ask me, "When was the house built?" I wouldn't say it was built on move-in day. It all started when the footings were laid, the rebar was fitted, and the concrete was poured. That was the beginning of the house. In the same way, Jesus' earthly ministry was laying the footings, tying the rebar, and pouring the foundation of the church that would ultimately take full shape with the coming of the Spirit at Pentecost. You can see this as you read the gospels. By the strictest definition, the church is a group of believers in Jesus Christ who have been called to follow him. That is exactly what the first followers of Jesus did. They each responded to Jesus' invitation to "follow me." They were followers of Jesus. They belonged to him. They possessed eternal life based on the work of Christ on the cross (John 10.14-16; 27-30). The functional ministries of the church also began with the first followers of Jesus. The followers of Jesus experienced forgiveness of sins (Luke 5.23; 7.48; John 10.28), lived in community (Mark 6.31; Acts 1.13-14), preached the gospel (Mark 3.13, 6.12), baptized believers (John 4.2), received the Lord's Supper (Matthew 26.26-29), worshipped Jesus (Matthew 14.33, 28.17; Luke 24.52), prayed (Luke 11.1-13; Acts 1.14), received the commission to spread the gospel (Matthew 28.18-20; Acts 1.8), exercised power over the demonic in Jesus' name (Mark 6.7), and experienced the moving of the Spirit (John 20.22) all prior to the day of Pentecost. Therefore, since Jesus' ministry to his church began with the calling of his disciples, the ministry of Jesus is the ministry of the local church. The apostles are described as the foundation of the church because they knew Jesus personally, were trained by Jesus, and carried on the work of Jesus as the church continued to grow and multiply. It's interesting to note that Paul, who fills in more details about church structure, leadership, and function, personally followed the pattern of ministry Jesus established (I Corinthians 11.1) and continued the disciple-making strategy of Jesus (2 Timothy 2.2). Jesus is the model of ministry for the church because Jesus is the head of the church (Colossians 1.18, Ephesians 5.23), the foundation of the church (Ephesians 2.20), and the builder of the church (Matthew 16.18).

**Misconception #4—Jesus lived in a different culture; it won't work today.**

Some leaders reject the disciple-making ministry of Jesus as the model for the local church for purely pragmatic reasons. They just don't think it will work. I don't know how many times I've talked to pastors about disciple making in their church and they give me a blank stare. Most are not sure what I'm talking about. For them, ministry in the modern day of technology, sophistication, and globalization means better buildings, better preaching, and better programs. They just don't think that one on one or small group disciple making will work today. I think the opposite. From what I've witnessed, all the models of the local church have not produced greater disciples for Jesus. They haven't produce more boldness, more holiness, more devotion. If anything, many of the ministries today dumb down the message of Jesus in order to placate those who fill the seats. Somehow we have convinced ourselves that greater attendance means greater ministry. Jesus, however, didn't fall for that. He didn't give himself to the crowds. He knew what was in the heart of men (John 2.24-25). He knew what people really need is a life-changing encounter with him. Somehow today we have more attending, but fewer transformed. More claim to know Jesus, but few live like they know Jesus. Jesus knew that life transformation happens when one person invests their life in another (I Thessalonians 2.8). That is what he did with his men. That is what he called his men to do, and that is what happened in the early church. Jesus started with five men (John 1.35-51). Over the next twelve months that number grew to twelve (Mark 3.13-14). Those twelve Jesus trained for about a year until they reproduced to seventy (Luke 10.1-24). While as many as five hundred believers were witness to his resurrection (I Corinthians 15.6), only one hundred twenty were truly committed to him and ready to ignite a movement (Acts 1.13-15). From that small group of committed disciples came an explosion for multiplication. Within two years they had "filled Jerusalem" with the gospel (Acts 5.28). Within four and a half years there were multiplying churches (Acts 9.30). In nineteen years they had "turned the world upside down" (Acts 17.6). Within twenty-eight years, the gospel had spread all over the known world (Colossians 1.56). Some may say, "Yes, I know that multiplication happened in the New Testament, but I don't think it happens today." If I could, I would introduce you my friend Harry Tembo. Harry lives in Lusaka, Zambia. Lusaka is the sprawling capital city of Zambia, an urban center teaming with well over two million people. Several years ago, a team from our church traveled to Zambia to invest in a handful of pastors and train them to make disciples like Jesus. Harry was part of that original group of pastors. To meet Harry is to love him. His small, thin frame and dark skin stand in stark contrast to his brilliant smile and larger than life personality. It was during that first training that Harry caught the vision of making disciples. His heart surged with excitement and he immediately began to invest his life in other pastors. Soon the handful of pastors began to multiply. More resources were printed, and more lives were impacted. Before long, these pastors were traveling into outlying areas, sharing the gospel, and investing their lives in emerging leaders. It was a rapidly moving, indigenous movement. Today the leaders in Zambia have grown to well over three thousand, establishing churches and training leaders. They also have a vision to build multiplying disciples in every nation south of the Sahara. God is at work. God works through his people as they give themselves fully to his commission to make disciples to the ends of the earth.

**Misconception #5—Jesus' plan is too hard and it takes too long.**

This may be the most honest complaint yet. The others are often theological smoke screens to hide a deeper problem. The fact is, most pastors are looking for something easy and immediate. Something that will get the numbers up, the people happy, the baptisms flowing, and the financials growing. Most pastors are overworked, under-resourced, and laden with the guilt of not leading well enough, not preaching well enough, or not getting the results they hope for. I can certainly relate to that.

If you measure your success in ministry and personal worth on how many attended your weekend services or how many baptisms you had last quarter, you are going to be on an emotional roller coaster. Let's just be brutally honest. Most churches in the United States aren't growing. According to a recent poll by Tom Rainer, only 6% of churches are actually growing. That means six out of one hundred are growing, and ninety-four have either plateaued or are declining.[5] This means that out of one hundred pastors reading this book, ninety-four of you are leading churches that are struggling. That's just reality. And that reality is troublesome. I remember talking over the phone with a pastor in a small community. I asked him how things were going. He paused for a while, then said, "I'm in a dying church in a dying town." I could feel the pain and frustration in his voice. We've all been there at some point. I remember leading the church in Oklahoma. I felt at times like the church was a huge boulder I was pushing up a hill, and if I relaxed for just a minute, it would come rolling down on top of me. I was looking for some answers—some quick answers. Look, I have some good news for you. Are you ready for it? I don't have any quick fixes or easy answers. There is no model that will instantaneously turn around a visionless department or fix an underperforming staff member or boost your offering next week or get rid of that cranky elder. What I do have is a plan that Jesus gave us, that will over time

---

5    www.churchleaders.com; *Seven Startling Facts: an up close look at church attendance in America.*

produce real, genuine, authentic, Christ-loving men and women. As I look back over the years of my ministry, my greatest source of joy hasn't come from accomplishing a certain goal or constructing a building. My joy is in the people I personally invested my life into and watching them continue to walk with God and make disciples. This is what Paul meant when he said, *"For what is our hope or joy or crown of boasting before our Lord Jesus at his coming? Is it not you?" (2 Thessalonians 2.19)*. Let me ask you a gut-level question. Who have you invested your life into? Could you write down on a piece a paper the names of people you have personally trained to walk with God, share their faith, and make disciples? If the answer is no, then you are missing out on the joy of ministry. Listen, the answer to the lack of volunteers in your church is more genuine, Spirit-empowered disciples. The answer to the conflict problems in your church is more genuine, Spirit-empowered disciples. The answer to your low evangelism fruit in your church is more genuine, Spirit-empowered disciples. The answer to your financial problems in your church is more genuine, Spirit-empowered disciples. The answer to just about any malady that makes the church weak and anemic is the need for more sold-out, fired-up, genuine, Spirit-empowered disciples. The way to get more disciples like this is to make them. One person at a time. And that starts with you. Over the next few chapters, I'm going to show you how to do just that. So let's put the excuses behind us. Let's agree that Jesus has a plan for his church and we need to get on that plan and stop chasing the latest model. If you can agree with that, then you are ready for the next bold move.

As I look back over the years of my ministry, my **greatest source of joy** hasn't come from accomplishing a certain goal or constructing a building. My joy is in **the people I personally invested my life into** and watching them continue to **walk with God** and make disciples.

Jesus never told us to build the church. **That's his job**. Jesus told us to **make disciples**. That's our job.

# MOVE FROM DECISIONS TO DISCIPLES

One afternoon, I was playing golf with a friend of mine who is a leading executive for a company that grosses over a billion dollars in revenue every year. I was talking non-stop about the church and some new initiatives I wanted to roll out, and I asked him for his input. As he addressed the ball to tee off on the next hole, he paused, looked up at me, and said, "Craig, you just need to determine how you define success. Then do the things that lead to success." He went back to work driving his ball down the fairway, but that statement sent my mind reeling. Sounds pretty simple doesn't it? Success for a coach is winning games. Success for a business is increased profits. Success for a school is higher test scores. But how do you define success in ministry? There are many metrics leaders use to define success: growing attendance, increased baptisms, rise in giving, more campuses, greater media market share, caring for the poor, championing justice, selling Christian resources, international outreach...the list could go on and on. But how did Jesus define success? After all, at the end of the day it is Jesus who will ultimately determine whether your ministry is successful or not. A businessman told me one time that he spent his whole life climbing the ladder of success only to discover it was leaned up against the wrong tree. He had been so focused on his career and financial success that he had neglected God's desire and plan for his life. When I think about church ministry and the way we measure success, sometimes I wonder if our ladder is leaning on the wrong tree. Is success in Jesus' eyes measured in numerical growth, financial stability, or creative worship? The church at Laodicea could have been a growing church running thousands in attendance, but they were so lukewarm it made Jesus sick and he was about to spit them out (Revelation 3.16). So, what is Jesus looking for in a healthy church?

Following his resurrection, Jesus gathered his faithful men on a mountain in Galilee (Matthew 28.16). I'm sure it was one they had visited many times before. I often take leaders to Israel to walk in the steps of Jesus. One prominent mountain on the northwest shore of the Sea of Galilee is Mount Arbel. While I'm not absolutely sure this was the mountain where Jesus met his disciples, it certainly could be. It has a distinct profile, with a protruding high peak and a steep drop off. This mountain stands out as unique among those encircling the Galilean lake. Also, it is strategically located along the Valley of the Doves connecting Nazareth to the Sea of Galilee. I'm sure Jesus and his disciples passed by this mountain many times. The last time I was there, I stood on top of this peak and looked out over Israel. On a clear day looking north you can see the borders of Syria and Lebanon. To the east you can see Ammon and the Decapolis, to the south the Jezreel Valley and the hills of Samaria, and to the west the port of Caesarea Maritima, where Roman ships transported the Apostle Paul and the gospel to the west. You can literally see the nations stretched out before you. I can just imagine Jesus standing there with his men, in his glorified body with arms wide open commissioning his disciples. *"All authority in heaven and on earth has been given to me. Go therefore and make disciples of all nations, baptizing them in the name of the Father and of the Son and of the Holy Spirit, teaching them to observe all that I have commanded you. And behold, I am with you always, to the end of the age"* (Matthew 28.18-20).

Buried in this final vision statement is Jesus' definition of success. There is only one command here, one verb. Jesus commanded his followers to make disciples. Circle it. Simply put, Jesus envisioned his church multiplying disciples that would reach every nation on the planet. Notice what Jesus did not say. He didn't say go plant churches. He didn't say go grow congregations. He didn't say go build buildings, produce resources, or increase revenue. Jesus never told us to build the church. That's his job. He told Peter plainly, "I will build my church" (Matthew 16.18). Jesus told us to make disciples. That's our job. Now, I'm not saying that planting churches or growing congregations is wrong. However, we can focus so much on church planting and church growth that we plant and grow churches filled with people who aren't true disciples of Jesus. We can have big churches filled with causal attendees and marginal believers who are not ever challenged to grow up and engage in Jesus' command to make disciples. I know this because it has happened before.

In 1662, the church in the New England colonies was struggling and in desperate need of revitalization. Many felt the spiritual fervor of the Colonists was fading and more people were pursuing material gain. Those that had made the arduous journey to establish the new nation as a "City on a Hill" were devoted Christians who envisioned a new nation established on the Bible and the rule of Christ. These leaders founded and established Congregational churches in New England. However, their children often did not follow the spiritual devotion of their parents. In an effort to keep these children in the church, a provision was made. The children of believing parents could be baptized and join the membership of the church, but could not partake of the Communion until they had professed faith in Christ. This was called the "Halfway Covenant." These unbelieving children were bound to the church through the covenant of their parents, but their full inclusion into the church was only halfway and dependent on their own profession of faith. The issue became even more problematic as these children of the "Halfway Covenant" had children of their own who were not Christians. Should this third generation be included in the church, even though they were children of unbelieving parents and hadn't expressed faith in Christ? This was the big debate. Some leaders such as the Reverend Solomon Stoddard believed that giving these people inclusion into the church would allow them to see the value of church membership and eventually they would respond to the gospel and be saved. Others strongly opposed including non-believers as members of the church, fearing that it would dilute the church of its purity and would eventually destroy the church from the inside out. By the time Jonathan Edwards (the grandson of Reverend Stoddard) was preaching at North Hampton during the First Great Awakening, the majority of the people in the church were unconverted. Over the long haul, the Halfway Covenant did what its dissenters feared. Today, the New England Congregational Church is in serious decline, and anyone can join without having to make a profession of faith in Jesus or be baptized. The Halfway Covenant is just one example of how churches have tried to make it easier for people to get into church, even at the expense of not knowing Jesus. Consequently, today in America we have declining mainline denominations that no longer hold to the authority of scripture or the gospel of salvation by faith in Christ alone.

In all our efforts to grow churches, we must be careful that we don't grow churches at the expense of making disciples. It was Jesus' vision that his church produce disciples. A successful church in Jesus' eyes is one that intentionally and strategically makes disciples and produces disciple makers. If that's true, then the next obvious question is, "What is a disciple?"

## WHAT IS A DISCIPLE?

Most pastors I talk to know instinctively that they need to be making disciples. But ask a group of pastors to define a disciple and you will get a huge variety of answers. Getting a solid biblical definition of a disciple is mission critical. The term "disciple" that Jesus used in Matthew 28.19 is the word *mathetes* which means "to learn." The Hebrew term for a disciple is *talmidim*, which also is derived from the word "to learn" and was used for a young man who left his home to study under a Rabbi. Therefore, a disciple is, at the core, a learner. But a disciple is more than that. A disciple is more than just a student or a person who acquires Biblical facts. To find out more, you have to dig deeply into the culture of the Old Testament because disciple making didn't start with Jesus. It pre-dates him.

Throughout the Old Testament you see spiritual leaders gathering disciples around them to train. One of the best examples of this is found in I Kings 19. Elijah was a mighty man of God. This was the man who faced off 450 prophets of Baal in front of the entire nation on Mount Carmel. This was the man who defied a king and ran from a queen. Elijah was the man who would eventually go up to heaven in a fiery chariot. Suffice it to say, he was an important guy. He was so important that when Jesus was preparing to go to the cross, on the mountain of transfiguration, only two men appeared there to encourage him—Moses and Elijah (Matthew 17.3). The prophet Malachi predicted that Elijah would come before the great and terrible day of the Lord (Malachi 4.5). But Elijah was a person just like you and me. James 5.17 tells us he got discouraged like we sometimes do. He had some great moments, some exhilarating mountain-top experiences, but he also had people after his head and threatening to bring him down. Every pastor can relate to this man. One minute he is calling fire from heaven, the next minute he's ready to call it quits. But in his darkest moments, God drew close to Elijah. Elijah traveled to Mount Horeb in the southernmost point of the Sinai Peninsula, and there God spoke to him. It is really an encouraging story because if you have ever felt like quitting or felt like a failure, this story proves that God cares about you more than your production or your bottom line. God has a purpose for you. He knows what you are feeling. He understands the times when your heart is tired and the seasons when ministry is hard. Two times God asked Elijah a simple question: "*What are you doing here Elijah?*" Each time Elijah rattled off his problems, the resistance he was facing, and the issues that were weighing him down. Elijah's face was buried in his troubles. God instructed Elijah to go out and stand before him. It was there that Elijah saw the power of God in a tornado which splintered the rocks. Elijah experienced the fury of God in a blazing fire. Elijah felt the might of God in a furious earthquake. But what Elijah needed to hear the most was the voice of God speaking to him. Let's pause right here. When ministry is hard and discouragement sets in like a dark cloud, the only cure is to be still enough to hear God's voice—to draw away long enough to lift your eyes from your problems and set your eyes on Jesus. Once that happens, then you are ready to hear God give you practical next steps to take in your ministry. Elijah set his face toward the Lord and tuned his ears to hear his voice. Then God gave him some instructions. I picture Elijah writing this all down so he doesn't forget.

"Return on your way to Damascus."

Check.

"Anoint Hazael to be king over Syria."

Got it.

"Anoint Jehu the son of Nimshi king over Israel."

Ok.

"Then anoint Elisha the son of Shaphat of Abel-meholah to replace you as prophet."

Roger that. Wait a minute. What was that again? Replace me?

The curtain was coming down on the days of Elijah and the curtain was about to rise on the ministry of Elisha. So Elijah did as the Lord instructed him. He anointed Hazael and Jehu, and made his way to the place where

Elisha lived. I love how the story unfolds. *"So he departed from there and found Elisha the son of Shaphat, who was plowing with twelve yoke of oxen in front of him, and he was with the twelfth. Elijah passed by him and cast his cloak upon him. And he left the oxen and ran after Elijah and said, 'Let me kiss my father and my mother, and then I will follow you.' And he said to him, 'Go back again, for what have I done to you?' And he returned from following him and took the yoke of oxen and sacrificed them and boiled their flesh with the yokes of the oxen and gave it to the people, and they ate. Then he arose and went after Elijah and assisted him."*

Elisha was working the fields as he had done since his youth. But God knew his address and he knew his potential. God instructed Elijah to "cast the mantle" of disciple making across Elisha's shoulders. In many ways, it is reminiscent of the way Jesus called his disciples, saying, *"Follow me and I will make you fishers of men"* (Matthew 4.18-19). Elijah called Elisha out to be trained, and Elisha was ready and willing. He said goodbye to his family and friends, cooked a barbeque with his cattle and plows, and set off to follow his master. When his time of training was completed, Elisha experienced a double portion of his master's strength and power (2 Kings 2.9, 14). Eventually Elisha carried on the work his master left behind for him to do. The prophets even declared, *"The spirit of Elijah rests on Elisha"* (2 Kings 2.15). The purpose of Elisha's training wasn't simply to learn facts about Elijah. The purpose of Elisha's training was to transform him in such a way that he became like his master so as to carry on the work. This is the heart and purpose of a true disciple maker. A disciple is more than a learner, he is a follower who is determined to become like his master and to carry on the work.

Throughout the Old Testament you see this model of disciple making. There were schools of prophets built around the disciple-making model (Isaiah 8.16). There were schools of musicians, trained for service in the temple (I Chronicles 25.8). Later there were Rabbinic schools established. The idea of disciple making is deeply rooted in the Old Testament. As you move into the gospels you see different kinds of disciples. There were "disciples of Moses" (John 9.28), disciples of the Pharisees (Matthew 22.16; Mark 2.18; Luke 5.33), "disciples of John the Baptist" (Matthew 9.14; Mark 2.18; Luke 5.33), and disciples of Jesus (Matthew 28.18-20). A disciple was a person who was close to a master, and followed that master to become like him and to carry on his work.

In the New Testament, the term "disciple" becomes synonymous with a "believer" in Jesus Christ. In Acts 4.32, "those who believe" are later referred to as "disciples" in Acts 6.2. A disciple had become synonymous with a believer (Acts 6.7; 9.26; 14.21-22). When you look at the gospels, the term disciple is the primary term used to describe a follower of Jesus. The term is used 261 times in the gospels and the Book of Acts.[6] Later, disciples

---

6    *Discipleship in the New Testament* by Robert Foster, Society of Biblical Literature, www.sbl.org.

of Jesus would be called "Christians" (Acts 11.26). As we move past the Book of Acts and into the epistles, the use of the term "disciple" begins to fade away and it is replaced with terms like "brother/sister," "saint," "believer," or "Christian."

# THE END PRODUCT

Clarifying and simplifying the definition of a disciple is critical if your church is going to be committed to making disciples. You can't have a fuzzy vision of your end product. That is what a disciple is—it's the end product of a church. Just as a tire factory produces tires or a computer factory builds computers, healthy churches make disciples. We need clear specs on what a disciple looks like, especially if Jesus is going to be the one evaluating the quality of our work (I Corinthians 3.12-13). The Apostle Paul was very clear on what he was trying to produce in the life of every person he met and every church he planted. See if you can pick up on Paul's end product. To the church at Rome he wrote; *"for those whom he foreknew he also predestined to be conformed to the image of his Son, in order that he might be the first born among many brothers"* (Romans 8.29). To the churches in Galatia he wrote, *"...I am again in the anguish of childbirth until Christ is formed in you!"* (Galatians 4.19). To the church at Corinth he wrote, *"But we Christians have no veil over our faces; we can be mirrors that brightly reflect the glory of the Lord. And as the Spirit of the Lord works within us, we become more and more like him"* (2 Corinthians 3.18, TLB). And to the church at Colossae he wrote, "*He is the one we proclaim, admonishing and teaching everyone with all wisdom, so that we may present everyone fully mature in Christ. To this end I strenuously contend with all the energy Christ so powerfully works in me*" (Colossians 1.28-29). In every church, with every person, Paul's goal was to see people become more and more like Jesus. He wanted people to be conformed to the image of Jesus, to be mirrors that reflect Jesus, to be matured into the likeness of Jesus. Paul's end product was Christ-like followers.

Over the years, I have used a 3D definition of a disciple. When you think of 3D, you think of something three-dimensional—fully orbed and lifelike. In the same way, a true disciple of Jesus has three dimensions that make him or her fully mature, fully orbed, and Christ-like.

## DEVOTED

The first dimension of a disciple is that they are devoted to Jesus. That is, this person has become convinced that Jesus is the Christ and that salvation is found in no one else but him. This is where disciple making begins. It begins when a person turns from their sin and turns to Jesus as the forgiver and the leader of their life. There is no disciple apart from conversion. Jesus modeled this for us. As he picked up the preaching mantle and began to lead the movement John the Baptist had begun, he started preaching a simple message. It only had two points: "Repent and believe" (Mark 1.15). I remember having coffee with a young man at a crowded Starbucks.

He had been attending a church for several years and was feeling an urge to go into vocational ministry. He asked if I would visit with him about it so we agreed to meet. As we settled into our seats I asked him about his spiritual journey and how God was moving in his life. He was a lean, sharp young man in his early twenties with a tight haircut, untucked shirt, and pressed shorts. He leaned forward, and with excitement in his voice spent the next half hour talking about how much he loved the people in the church and how he really enjoyed serving in the church youth group. I listened intently. Then, while drawing my cup up close for another sip I said, "So, tell me when you gave your life to Christ." He paused and looked at me as if he didn't understand the question, so I rephrased. "I mean, tell me when you became a Christian. How did that happen?" He mumbled something along the lines of, "I've always believed in God. I was confirmed at the age of twelve," but he was obviously grasping for words. That night, I spent my time talking to him about Jesus. I shared with him how much God loves him and that God created him to know Him in a deep and personal way. I explained that our problem is that sin has separated us from God and we are all cut off from him. I remember saying, "Look around this crowded coffee shop." His eyes scanned the room, briefly glancing at the faces of the people standing in line to order. "Everyone in this room, and everyone in our world has fallen short of God's design for them. Everyone of us is separate from God and helplessly lost." I could see his demeanor change as he absorbed the heaviness of those words. I continued, "But that is why Jesus came. God sent His only son, Jesus, to die on a cross. On that cross, he absorbed the wrath of God for us and paid the penalty of sin on our behalf. He died. He was buried. Three days later he rose again, conquering sin and death and the grave. If you will turn from your sin and turn to Jesus, he promises to forgive you and restore your broken relationship with God." I let the words hang in the air. Then I asked, "Have you ever done that?" After a good while, he simply said, "No, I haven't." In fact, he wasn't sure he was ready for that kind of commitment. Going to seminary was one thing, but actually following Jesus was altogether different. As we left that coffee shop, I wondered how many other people are just like this young man—churched, involved, and sincere, but lost. The first step in becoming a disciple is coming to faith in Jesus. Paul put it simply: *"If you confess with your mouth that Jesus is Lord and believe in your heart God that raised him from the dead, you will be saved"* (Romans 10.9). A biblical conversion involves an acknowledgment of my sin before God, a belief that Jesus is the Son of God and only his death and resurrection can pay for my sin, and a turning from my sin and turning to Jesus in simple faith. This is what Jesus meant when he said, "You must be born again" (John 3.7). Just like you are born into your earthly family, in the same way you must be born into God's family. That happens through placing your faith in Jesus. Nicodemus was a religious man. He knew Bible facts. He was devoted to ritual and tradition as a Jewish Rabbi. Jesus told him, *"Unless one is born again he cannot see the kingdom of God"* (John 3.3). A true disciple is one who is devoted to Jesus and has been born into God's family through faith in Jesus.

# DEVELOPING

The second dimension of a disciple is that he is progressively developing the character and the competencies of Jesus in his own life. Remember, a disciple is one who follows a master in order to become like him. Accordingly, a disciple of Jesus is someone who has chosen to follow Jesus and is in the process of becoming more and more like him. Theologians call this sanctification. It's the process by which the Spirit of God begins to mold and shape the new believer into the image of Christ. Jesus prayed this for each of his disciples. The night before his death he prayed, *"Father, they are not of the world even as I am not of the world. Sanctify them by your truth; your word is truth"* (John 17.16-17). The word "sanctification" (*hagiazon*) means to be separate or set apart. Just as Jesus was set apart for a redemptive purpose to ignite a global disciple-making movement, so his followers have been "born from above" (John 3.3) and have been set apart to join Jesus in his mission (John 20.21). That involves walking as Jesus walked (I John 2.6) and doing what Jesus did (John 14.12).

There are two primary areas where a disciple needs to develop.

First, a disciple must develop the character of Jesus. This is Christ-likeness on the inside. Paul was referring to this when he urged the Philippians to, *"Let each of you look not only to his own interests, but also to the interests of others. Have this mind among yourselves, which is yours in Christ Jesus..." (Philippians 2.4-5).* The word mind (*phroneo*) means to think in the same way or have the same disposition or attitude. Paul was encouraging these new believers to have the same attitude, thoughts, character, and internal disposition as Jesus. He just mentioned a few ways they could do that; by being like-minded, not looking out for their own interests, caring for the interests of others, and considering others more important than themselves. All these are attitudes reflected in the life of Jesus. What are the character qualities of Jesus? You probably can't get a better list to start with than in Galatians 5.22-23. *"But the fruit of the Spirit is love, joy, peace, patience, kindness, goodness, faithfulness, gentleness, self-control..."* These are called the "fruit of the Spirit," but they were perfectly lived out in the life of Jesus. He expressed ultimate love and joy. He exemplified peace and patience in all circumstances. He modeled kindness to the forgotten, goodness to the wayward, faithfulness to the faltering, and gentleness and self-control in even the worst of situations. A disciple is growing in these areas. He is learning, day by day, to let the Spirit of God control him, change him, and lead him.

He's not who he used to be. Is he perfect? Not even close. Is he making progress? Absolutely.

The second area of growth for the new disciple is developing the competencies of Jesus. This is Christ-likeness on the outside. When Jesus called his disciples to "follow him" he trained them to be like him and to carry on his work. For this to happen they needed to have certain competencies mastered. Think about it this way. When a master electrician trains a new apprentice, his goal is to make that novice competent in every area of their new job. There are certain skills they need to master. There are certain problems they need to solve. There is a certain baseline of knowledge they will need to have to carry on the work. In the same way, Jesus trained his men in certain competencies so they could carry on the work he had begun. You may be asking, "In what kind of competencies did Jesus train his disciples?" As you read through the gospels, some come quickly to the surface. For instance, Jesus trained his disciples in God's Word. Throughout the gospels, Jesus quoted the scriptures over seventy different times. He quoted scripture when he was tempted, when he was confronting the Pharisees, and as he taught. In every way, Jesus was training his men to understand God's Word. Jesus also trained his men how to pray. He often retreated by himself to seek his Father's face. Sometimes he would pray all night long before big decisions or when facing the heavy pressures of ministry. At least twice, we see Jesus teaching his disciples how to pray. Jesus also trained his men to communicate the gospel. He was called a friend of sinners (Luke 7.34). He cared for people far from God, not because they were a project, but because they mattered to God. He modeled personal and public evangelism and then sent his disciples out to do the same. Jesus also trained his men to invest their lives in others. Jesus prioritized relationships, choosing to invest the majority of his time in a few emerging leaders rather than give all of his attention to the clamoring crowd. In this way, Jesus was training his men to invest in others for optimal impact. These are just a few of the competencies Jesus developed in his disciples. The true disciple of Jesus is progressively growing in these competencies, as well. He's learning to carve out time for prayer and God's Word. He is intentionally building relationships with people far from God and sharing the gospel. He is investing his life in a few people and showing them how to walk with God. When people don't know what to do, they do nothing. But when a person is shown how to walk with God, then he is empowered to walk with God his whole life and help others do the same. I am forever grateful to the men who trained me in these things.

Jerry was one of three businessmen who discipled me when I was a young pastor. He owned his own business building runways for the government all across the United States. Jerry was a passionate disciple maker. He would often say, "Craig, left to ourselves we can never live the Christian life. It's impossible. We can't make ourselves change on the inside, no matter how much willpower we have. What we need is someone from the outside to come to us and change us on the inside. And that someone is Jesus. The way to live the Christian life is by being Christ-centered and Christ-controlled. Each day we make the choice to either acknowledge Jesus as the center of our lives around which everything else revolves, or put ourselves in that place. Every day we make the choice to either voluntarily surrender the control of our lives to Jesus, or to grab the reigns and assume control." I've never forgotten Jerry's words. Over the years, there have been times when I lived Christ-centered and Christ-controlled. In those moments, the Spirit of God produced in me the character of Jesus and a desire to live out the competencies of Jesus. But honestly, there have been days when Jesus hasn't been the center of my life. I've been busy working out my plans, my ways, my efforts. On those days Jesus hasn't been in control of my life. The result is that I give very little thought to the character and competencies of Jesus. We've all got room to grow. I'm not saying that a disciple has all of this down, but what I am saying is that a true disciple of Jesus is moving in this direction. The Spirit within him is working on him, and his desire is to live just like Jesus. The Apostle Paul told his young disciple, Timothy, *"Practice these things, immerse yourself in them, so that all may see your progress"* (I Timothy 4.15). The key word is progress! He didn't say, "Timothy you have to be perfect. You must have it all together all the time." He just said—keep moving forward. That was Paul's goal even for himself. I love how the

Apostle Paul put it: *"Not that I have already obtained this or am already perfect, but I press on to make it my own, because Christ Jesus has made me his own"* (Philippians 3.12). Paul wasn't perfect. He hadn't reached full maturity. He hadn't planted his flag on the mountaintop of Christ-likeness, but he was pressing toward it. He was making progress. His desire was to be like Jesus on the inside and on the outside. And that is the desire of every true disciple.

## DEPLOYED

The final dimension of a true disciple is deployment. True disciples are engaged in the ministry of Jesus. More specifically, they are making disciples by reaching the lost and investing in a few. Deployed is an action word. It's boots on the ground. Over the years I've had several friends who were in the military. One friend was a Commander in the Air Force during Operation Desert Storm. He flew several sorties into enemy territory during that conflict. For him, deployment means to leave the safety of home and engage in the battle. The true disciple is a deployed disciple. He isn't just someone who believes in Jesus and spends his time working on spiritual disciplines. He is actively advancing the kingdom of God by reaching people for Christ and walking with them to maturity. He has skin in the game. One day as Jesus was traveling from village to village, teaching and ministering to the crowds, he was overcome with compassion. He saw that they were *"harassed and helpless, like sheep without a shepherd"* (Matthew 9.36). The word harassed (*skullo*) means to be mangled, torn apart, and cut to the bone. The word helpless (*rhipto*) means to throw to the ground. Jesus saw these people the way his Father saw them—victims of the enemy. They were hurt, betrayed, abused, torn apart, beat down, discarded, and walked on. He saw that they had no one to look after them or care for them. I've seen my share of hurting people. I've walked through the slums in India where children were playing on garbage heaps, subsisting without clean water or shelter. I've been in inner-city schools, tagged and marked by the local gangs. I've looked into the eyes of the homeless, the single mom, the elderly and forgotten. During the economic recession of 2008-2009, the United States job market lost 8.4 million jobs. That represents 6.1% of all jobs in the nation. The area I'm serving was hit especially hard. I'll never forget seeing a middle-aged man standing on a street corner dressed in a nice suit and tie, briefcase at his side, holding a handwritten sign that read, "I need a job." Harassed. Helpless. Jesus was broken for these people. When I stop long enough to see people the way God does, my heart breaks, too. And in that moment of honest emotion, Jesus called for the solution. What's the solution to the pain and heartbreak in our culture? Jesus said, *"The harvest is plentiful, but the laborers are few, therefore pray earnestly to the Lord of the harvest to send out laborers into his harvest"* (Matthew 9.37). Jesus said the answer to human suffering in the world is prayer. But not a prayer that says, "Lord, help these people.

They are really hurting." It's a prayer that says, "Lord, help these people by sending more laborers into the harvest field." We often hear this verse when someone is making an earnest plea for more volunteers at the church. The children's workers are running low, so the pastor quotes this passage—"Pray earnestly for the Lord of the harvest to send laborers"—and the signup sheet is at the information desk as you exit the auditorium. But Jesus isn't telling us to pray for people to volunteer within the church. He's telling us to pray for people to be sent out from the church and into the harvest field. The harvest is where lost people are. The harvest is where people are hurting, where they are harassed and helpless and need the hope of the gospel. True disciples are deployed into the harvest field. They intentionally and purposefully seek out those who they know are far from God and they invest their lives in a few. Many disciples today are doing just this, even in the face of hostility and resistance. On a trip to Bangalore, India, I had the opportunity to sit with pastors who have suffered greatly to follow Jesus. We gathered in an upstairs cinder-block building. Fifteen to twenty Indian pastors sat politely in the seats, excited to hear what our team had to say to them. A local denominational leader who wanted to encourage pastors in his district organized the meeting. I was the scheduled preacher for the day, but I quickly realized that I was sitting among giants. Every one of these men had come from a Muslim background and had chosen to follow Christ at the risk of his life. One pastor heard the gospel in his remote village over a radio broadcast. He wrote in requesting a Bible, and for months he studied it in secret. When he was discovered to be a Christ follower, the village men beat him severely and threatened his life. His mother helped him to escape. He left behind his wife, children, home, and job. He had absolutely nothing. I also had the opportunity to meet a young woman named Fatima. When her family learned that she was a Christ follower, she was threatened with death—honor killing. She later escaped and found refuge with Christians. In the years that followed, she married a Christian young man and had a small child. Over time, she was able to communicate with her father and mother, and their hostility toward her seemed to subside. But when she returned home to retrieve some personal documents, her brothers beat her and her husband. As she told me her story, I could still see her bruises and the blood in her eyes. Jesus warned his followers that deployment into the harvest field wouldn't be easy, but he promised that he would be with them. Can you imagine a cadre of men and women in your church, trained and mobilized to reach people with the gospel and invest in new believers? Jesus could. That was his vision for his church. It still is.

So, let's review our definition of a disciple. A true disciple is a person who is devoted to Jesus, is developing the character and competencies of Jesus, and is deployed into the ministry of Jesus by reaching the lost and investing in a few. Jesus wanted 3D disciples.

## DECISION OR DISCIPLES?

When I look at that definition of a disciple, it seems a bit overwhelming. How do we make people like that? In most churches today, we have lowered the bar to something more manageable and realistic. Instead of making disciples, we focus on making decisions. In 2007, I left Oklahoma and moved back to Texas to pastor a large church in the heart of the Dallas/Fort Worth metroplex. When I arrived, one of the major evangelistic initiatives of the church involved a ministry to the local Hispanic community. Every year, prior to Christmas, the church would host people on the church campus. Guests would sit through a brief service where the gospel was presented. Then they would file into another building where they could shop for new Christmas toys. Church members would then wrap the toys and the guests would leave with free Christmas gifts. The church underwrote the project every year to the tune of over $100,000. My first year, I observed the finely-tuned machine. Our members were loving and serving each family that came onto the property. The next year, I suggested that an Hispanic evangelist present the gospel and we saw phenomenal results. Over 3,500 guests visited our campus, 250 made public professions of faith, and 40 were baptized on the spot! The Baptist Press featured a story about our evangelistic success. Everything was great. The next week I went out with a small team to visit with those who had prayed to receive Christ. We walked the apartments and trailer parks on the outskirts of our community. After days of knocking on doors and countless conversations, the results were in. There was not one person who had made a decision for Christ who wanted to continue their spiritual journey. We did not retain one person as a member of our church. We did not retain one person in a Bible study. We did not build one relationship that lasted. We did not retain one person for anything. Most said they prayed to receive Christ but had no interest in baptism or being involved in a church, period. We made lots of decisions, but no disciples.

Be honest. How much money and effort have you put into making decisions that were wasted because there was no lasting fruit? This is the dirty little secret of many churches and denominations. If you disagree, just ask yourself why so many churches post high baptism numbers, but their attendance remains flat or in decline. How can you be reaching people and not growing? In some cases, the back door to the church is as wide as the front door. But my hunch is that the front door isn't as wide as we think because those who made decisions quickly faded away. Jesus said there would be many who claim to follow Jesus but just don't. In the parable of the sower, Jesus said some seeds fell on the path and were quickly eaten up by the birds. Some seed fell on the rocky ground and sprouted quickly, but had no root. In the heat of day, it withered and died. That describes many decisions. They hear the word, and they respond quickly without counting the cost. They raise their hand, check the box, walk the aisle, but in a few weeks they are nowhere to be found. They didn't put down roots and their faith, when put to the test, didn't stand.

There is an inherent danger in focusing on making decisions over making disciples. When you focus on making decisions, you can easily manipulate people to inflate evangelistic numbers. We have all probably seen this to some degree in local churches and evangelistic meetings. Long, drawn out invitations. Emotional appeals. One event I witnessed asked children to raise their hands if they wanted to be "Jesus' forever friend," then counted each hand as a decision for Christ. When you are just making decisions, the end justifies the means. When you focus on making disciples, the pressure is off for an immediate decision and the emphasis is on presenting the gospel clearly and helping each person come to Jesus in a genuine way.

When you focus on making decisions, impersonal methods are used to boost numbers. Large gatherings, mass responses, herded decisions. Even one-on-one presentations of the gospel are more like cold call presentations to strangers rather than honest conversations between friends. When you focus on making disciples, you work in the context of relationships, so you actually know the person you are seeking to reach and you stay in a relationship with them as they continue their spiritual journey.

When you focus on making decisions, you have a tendency to rush the process that the Holy Spirit has begun in that person's life. Your goal is the decision.

When you focus on making disciples, you are willing to let people process the gospel until they are prepared to choose Christ in an authentic way.

When you focus on making decisions, you can develop a false sense of success. If the number of decisions is up, you can think you are truly winning people to Christ and even making disciples, even though the quality of the decision is suspect. When you focus on making disciples, you have a long-term perspective. Real success is counted when those who make decisions are walking in community, growing in their faith, and able to lead others to Christ.

When you focus on making decisions, your job is over after the decision is made. People are often dropped quickly or even forgotten. When you focus on making disciples, your job just begins when a person crosses the line of faith. They are spiritual babes that need nurturing, care, and protection.

## WHAT I'M NOT SAYING....

I'm not saying that all evangelism efforts are bad or a waste of time. As a pastor, I'm constantly stoking the fires of evangelism in our church. We are always working hard to reach as many people as we can with the message of life. I am not advocating taking the foot off the accelerator when it comes to sharing the gospel. What I am saying is that evangelism is only the first step in the disciple-making process. Anytime that evangelism is wrenched out of the context of a larger disciple-making strategy, it can quickly deteriorate into manipulation, gimmicks, and scrounging for decisions that seldom last. True evangelism will always result in true disciples. Anything that doesn't isn't real evangelism. For generations, there has been a great divide between the "evangelism camp" and the "discipleship camp" in churches. Some focus primarily on winning the lost, even if it means abandoning the new believers to fend for themselves. People have said to me, "I just win them, someone else can take care of them!" Others prefer deeper life teachings and focus primarily on spiritual formation and disciplines, even if it means that they seldom, if ever, share their faith. One woman plainly told me, "I'm not into evangelism, I just do discipleship." This problem isn't only in our churches. Even many of our denominations are divided on the organizational chart into evangelism departments and discipleship departments. The two are viewed as polar opposites, even at times seen as competitors for resources and focus, but Jesus never drew this distinction. Jesus wasn't *only* about evangelism and he wasn't *only* about discipleship. Jesus was *only* about making disciples. Making a disciple requires that you help people come to faith in Christ *and* train them to feed themselves and reproduce. It's not either/or, it's both.

Now more than ever we need churches that are not fixated on short-term gimmicks to achieve explosive numerical growth. What we need are churches that are committed to a long-term strategy to make disciples who will make disciples to the third and fourth generation. If you do that, the growth will take care of itself. I recently had the opportunity to sit down and visit with Pastor Peter Lord. Pastor Lord was born in Kingston, Jamaica, British West Indies. He later came to the United States for school and pastored Park Avenue Baptist Church in Titusville, Florida, for more than thirty years. Lord is a gifted speaker and author, best known for teaching people how to pray and hear God's voice. Today, Dr. Lord is retired and well into his 80s, and I wanted to hear words of wisdom from his life and ministry. We talked about a lot of things, his wit and sense of humor still sharp and surprising. When I asked him about the condition of the local church today, he got serious. Leaning forward and locking in on my eyes, he said, "England had the greatest preachers, but now they have empty cathedrals. We must do more than preach, we must make disciples." When I asked him what he would do differently if he could do ministry all over again, he said simply, "In my day, ministry was all about making decisions for Christ, but if I were doing it all again, I would make more disciples." Today Dr. Lord meets with people in his home and he trains them to walk with God, reach the lost, and invest in a few. He's making disciples.

Like Esau, **we have sold the birthright** Jesus gave us of building disciples **for the promise of church growth** and immediate success. We are now discovering that those methodologies are porridge, **ineffective to reach the next generation**.

# MOVE FROM PROGRAMS TO PROCESS

How do you make disciples?

I love asking pastors that question. Not long ago, I sat around a conference table with several pastors, professors, and denominational leaders. We were all there to talk about discipleship. When the question was asked about how disciples are made, the thoughts were pretty vague and varied. Most said that getting people into small groups made disciples. In these groups men and women were "being discipled." But when pressed to give specifics of how they knew discipling was taking place or what the end product looked like, the room got pretty quiet. In most cases, church leaders are running long-standing programs with little thought to whether these programs are actually contributing to the formation of passionate, reproducing disciples. If more people are in these programs year over year, it is a success. If attendance is waning, it is time for an overhaul or a new program. The question of whether or not the program is actually producing disciples is seldom asked. So, how do you make disciples in a local church?

I have to confess, I have a personal frustration regarding this issue. Most of the finely-tuned disciple-making ministries are found in the para-church world, not the local church, and that really bothers me. Great organizations like The Navigators, Campus Crusade, Youth with a Mission, Student Mobilization, Christian Businessmen's Committee, and others have a laser focus on making disciples and producing disciple makers. They have boards and leaders committed to making disciples. They have staff that spend every waking breath leading people to Christ and helping them grow in their faith. They see rapid rates of multiplication and they deploy people into other campuses, cities, and countries to make disciples for Christ. But when I look at the average church, I don't see any of that. I see churches gathering for worship and running programs with little thought or intentionality other than for numerical growth. Jesus loved the church. Jesus started the church. Jesus gave the Great Commission to the church. The early church was a disciple-making machine. Yet the local church today has almost abandoned Jesus' heart for disciple making. Like Esau, we have sold the birthright Jesus gave us of building disciples for the promise of church growth and immediate success. We are now discovering that those methodologies are porridge, ineffective to reach the next generation. We have been duped into thinking that large numbers equate to successful ministry. We have failed to play the role of the farmer who cultivates, plants, and waters, patiently praying until the fruit comes. My heart's desire is to see pastors in the local church reclaim their God-given legacies of disciple making. Call me crazy, but I think God designed the church to be the perfect place for making disciples. And I do think that as the church makes disciples, it becomes the hope of the world. For that to happen, we have to go back to the example of Jesus and replicate Jesus' disciple-making model.

## WHAT IT IS, WHAT IT'S NOT

Recently, I was in a meeting with several national disciple-making leaders. Most of these men and women have given their lives to making disciples and have written extensively on the subject. Many have thriving international ministries today. The purpose of the meeting was to discuss the status of disciple making in America. As the dialogue ensued, it became clear that there were differences of opinion on how disciple making should be done. At one point, Bill Hull made the statement, "We are using the same words but speaking a different language." I think the same is true when I talk to pastors about making disciples. We all agree we should make disciples, and in many cases we are using the same words, but behind those words are different meanings. The biggest struggle for clarity is the difference between "discipleship" and "disciple making." Today, when a leader uses the word discipleship, they usually mean spiritual growth that happens post-conversion. Discipleship is the next step after a person comes to faith in Christ. Recently, this definition was underscored by a study on discipleship by the George Barna research group. In their 2015 "State of Discipleship," commissioned by NavPress and The Navigators, the Barna Group interviewed 600 pastors and 2,000 practicing and non-practicing Christians. Discipleship was clearly defined as "the process of growing spiritually." Interestingly, only one-quarter of those surveyed thought the term "discipleship" was even relevant today, preferring terms such as "spiritual growth" or "spiritual journey."[7] Discipleship today is clearly seen as how a person grows spiritually. In this way, discipleship is distinguished from evangelism. "Evangelism is leading people to Christ, discipleship is growing people in Christ," they would say. Here, evangelism is seen as completely separate from discipleship. Carl Wilson, in his great book on disciple making, traces this thought back to the mid-1800s and points to a man named Charles Adams. Adams, a Methodist pastor who was born in New Hampshire in 1808 and died in 1890, authored many books, but his most recognized work was entitled, "Evangelism in the Middle of the Nineteenth Century." In his book, Adams

---

7    Barna.org *New Research on the State of Discipleship.*

meticulously records the status of evangelism around the world during his lifetime. According to Wilson, Adams was one of the first men to coin the phrase "evangelism," thus creating a seminal difference between evangelism and discipleship.[8] What was a hairline fracture in the 1800s has now become a great chasm in the new millennium. It is not uncommon for people and organizations to distinguish between "evangelism and discipleship" as I stated in the previous chapter. Therefore, discipleship is relegated to anything that helps people to grow. Pastors tell me, "We do discipleship in our worship services, small groups, accountability groups, Bible studies, men's and women's groups, church activities, and even online individual studies." Just about anything that promotes spiritual growth is thrown in the bucket of discipleship. Some have even told me, "Our discipleship is just hanging out and doing life together." Now you may be thinking, "What's wrong with that?" The problem is that this kind of discipleship is very different from the idea of making disciples that Jesus had in mind. First, discipleship is about a part of the process (what happens after a person is saved), where disciple making involves the whole process from leading a person to Christ to sending them out to reproduce. Disciple making begins with evangelism, includes new believers into the church, trains them to walk with God, and sends them out to reproduce

---

8    Carl Wilson, *With Christ is the school of Disciple Building*, Worshipwide discipleship Association books, Fayetteville, Georgia, 1976, page 219.

their lives in others. Second, discipleship usually doesn't have an end in mind. Most leaders cannot articulate an end product, as we have previously discussed. Disciple making has a clear end goal in mind. You are building a disciple that looks and acts like Jesus. Third, discipleship is usually heavily knowledge-based, where disciple making is heavily practice-based. The person is not just learning more things about Jesus in a Bible study, they are being trained to think, live, and walk like Jesus in their everyday lives. Fourth, discipleship usually ends when the Bible study is complete. Disciple making is focused on spiritual multiplication to the third and fourth generation. Jesus didn't just gather his men and hang out with them. He didn't just teach them and do service projects with them. Jesus was intentionally training his men to become like him so that he could release them into the world to carry on the movement. I think the church would be better served jettisoning the term "discipleship" and embracing the more biblical term and philosophy of disciple making.

## HOW DID JESUS DO IT?

Let's go back up to the mountain in Galilee. Jesus is casting his global vision to his few disciples. He said, "All authority has been given to Me in heaven and on earth. Go therefore and make disciples of all the nations, baptizing them in the name of the Father and the Son and the Holy Spirit, teaching them to observe all that I commanded you; and lo, I am with you always, even to the end of the age" (Matthew 28.18-20). As we have already seen, embedded in this vision statement is the purpose of the church—make disciples. The church exists to make disciples. But also embedded in this statement is the process of how to make disciples. This is incredible and serves to underscore the brilliance of Jesus. In one sentence he summarizes the product and the process! So, what's the process? Jesus taught that making disciples involves four clear steps.

The first step is to engage spiritual explorers with the gospel of Jesus. As we have already stated, evangelism is the first step in the disciple-making process. Jesus' phrase "go make disciples" is better read as "make disciples as you are going." An evangelist told me once, "You can't spell gospel without spelling go." I like that. As you are going along your normal pathways of life, make disciples. The gospel and disciple making in the early church ran clearly along relational lines. The Greek word "oikos" is used repeatedly in the New Testament. It is translated "household," but also was used in a broader sense to include extended family, friends, co-workers, and neighbors. The early church grew rapidly because they took the good news of Jesus back to their "oikos." When Jesus healed a man possessed by demons he told him to go back and share the good news with his family (*oikos*) (Mark 5.19). When Zacchaeus came to faith in Christ, Jesus declared that salvation had come to his house (*oikos*) (Luke 19.9). So, disciple making begins with going to your established relationships and telling them about Jesus (see also John 1.40, 4.53; Mark 2.14; Acts 10.1-2; 16.14-15, 30-34).

The second step in the process is to connect new believers into a biblical community. Jesus said that new disciples were to be baptized *"in the name of the Father and of the Son and of the Holy Spirit."* Baptism not only identified the person as a follower of Jesus, but also included him in the new community of believers where he could grow and be nurtured in the faith. The third step is to grow disciples and disciple makers by training them to walk with God. Jesus said these disciples are to be taught to obey him in everything. *"Teaching them to observe all that I have commanded you…"* (Matthew 28.20). In this phase, the disciple is trained to walk with God on their own and to begin to develop the character and competencies of Jesus. I Timothy 4.7 says, *"train yourself to be godly."* Paul said that just as the athlete *"goes into strict training"* to get a temporary crown, he disciplines himself for an eternal reward (I Corinthians 9.25). This phase of equipping and training involves discipline. It includes learning to feed yourself by reading God's Word and learning to cultivate a personal relationship with Jesus through prayer. It involves learning to share your faith and reflect the love of God and Christ to the people around you. It involves learning to trust Jesus with every circumstance of life and put him first in everything.

The fourth and final step is not clearly stated in this passage, but is implied. Jesus said that the new disciple was to obey everything he commanded, which includes the command to "go make disciples." Jesus intended for disciples to make disciples. The fourth step, therefore, is

3. MOVE FROM PROGRAMS TO PROCESS

to release this new disciple to multiply his life in the life of others. Before his death, Jesus told his men, *"By this my Father is glorified, that you bear much fruit and so prove to be my disciples" (John 15.8).* Things that are mature, multiply. A mature plant bears fruit. A mature animal produces offspring. A mature follower of Jesus multiplies disciples. That's what happened in the early church. Acts 6.7 states *"...the Word of God continued to increase and the number of disciples multiplied greatly in Jerusalem...."* Jesus gave us a clear product: make disciples. He also gave us a clear process: engage explorers, connect believers, grow disciples, and go multiply. But he also gave us a wonderful promise. He said, "If you make it your goal to make disciples and you follow the four-step process I have given you, then I will be with you. Always. To the very end of the age." That's an incredible promise for you and me. When you are committed to making disciples the way Jesus did, you will never lack his presence or his power!

## THE PROCESS

Before we dive into the details of how Jesus put this process to work, let me make a few observations about the process itself. First, as you've noticed, the process is linear (see Appendix). People move from one stage to the next as they develop. This is the natural way things grow. When you look at a stalk of wheat, it grows in a predictable pattern. First the seed, then the root, then the stalk, and finally the head. Jesus understood this process of natural growth (Mark 4.28-29). When you look at people, they grow physically in predictable patterns as well. When our girls were born, it all started with a sonogram. Even in the womb the doctors were measuring every part of their growth and development. My wife even had a book that described with pictures how the baby was developing at every week in the pregnancy. After each birth we would take them to the pediatrician for regular check ups, and again they would rank their growth percentiles. I'm so competitive, I celebrated when they were in the 100% category! Every person is different, but every person grows physically in the same way. The same is true spiritually. Every person is different, but every person grows in Christ-likeness the same way, passing through the same stages of spiritual maturity. The second observation is that the process is a supernatural work of God! I can't force people to grow spiritually any more than I can force someone to grow physically. The Apostle Paul, talking about spiritual growth said, *"I planted, Apollos watered, but God gave the growth. So neither he who plants nor he who waters is anything, but only God who gives the growth"* (I Corinthians 3.6). Two times he stated that it was God who caused the growth. We can plant seeds of faith, but only God can turn a heart toward him. We can reach out in love, but only God can build a community. We can invest in a person's life, but only the Spirit can take that investment and bring transformation. We can challenge, model, resource, and ask people to multiply, but only God can burden their hearts to go make disciples.

To the Colossians, Paul wrote, *"He is the one we proclaim, admonishing and teaching everyone with all wisdom, so that we may present everyone fully mature in Christ. To this end I strenuously contend with all the energy Christ so powerfully works in me"* (Colossians 1.28-29). Paul did his part of admonishing and teaching. It was strenuous work. But at the end of the day, he did it all through the power and energy of the Spirit of Christ working through him. Ultimately it is all God's doing, making people into new creations (Philippians 2.13; 2 Corinthians 5.17) and we are completely dependent on Him to move and work in the hearts of people. In fact, it's up to us to sense where God is working and join him, just as Jesus did. In John 5.17 Jesus said, *"My Father is always at his work to this very day, and I too am working."* Finally, it is the job of the pastors and leaders of the church to keep the process in the forefront of the church. If Jesus commanded that we make disciples this way, then we need to do it the way Jesus said to do it. I have a good friend who likes to say, "Jesus started the church the way he wanted it. Now he wants it the way he started it." We don't have the luxury or the authority to change what Jesus has mandated. We are simply called to shepherd the flock under our care, with the right motives under the leadership of Jesus, the Chief Shepherd who is coming back for his church (I Peter 5.1-4). With that in mind, let's dig deeper into how Jesus moved people through this process.

## PHASE ONE: ENGAGE EXPLORERS

One day Jesus was sitting on a mountain, overlooking the sprawling Jezreel Valley that spread out like a patchwork quilt in front of him. For the past eighteen years, he had been faithfully working in his earthly father's trade as a craftsman. As the firstborn son it was his job to provide for the family. He had also been faithfully preparing for the day when his heavenly Father would give him a sign that the time was right for his ministry to begin. Today was that day. Jesus heard his Father's voice to go and be baptized by his cousin, John. Jesus left his hometown of Nazareth in northern Galilee and made the sixty mile, two-day trek south along the Jordan River valley to Bethel beyond the Jordan just north of the Dead Sea (John 1.28). There, he was baptized and immediately thrust by the Spirit into the rocky and dry Judean wilderness to be tempted for forty days (Luke 4.1-13). When his time of testing was complete, Jesus returned to where John was preaching and baptizing. John saw Jesus and pointed him out for everyone to see. *"Behold the Lamb of God who takes away the sin of the world"* (John 1.29). The next day it happened again. John pointed out Jesus declaring, *"Behold, the Lamb of God!"* (John 1.35). This time, two of John's followers peeled off and started following Jesus. Sensing he was being followed, Jesus turned and asked these men, *"What are you seeking?"* I'm sure they were caught off guard by Jesus' direct question. They replied, *"Rabbi* (which means teacher) *where are you staying?"* Jesus said, *"Come and you will see"* (John 1.38-39). That day was a turning point for these men. By the end of the day, they were convinced that Jesus was the Christ, the Messiah sent from God. One of these men, named Andrew, quickly found his brother, Peter and said, *"We have found the Messiah!"* (John 1.42). The next day Jesus found Philip, a hometown friend of Andrew and Peter, and called him to be his follower (John 1.43). Then Philip found a friend of his, Nathanael, and he pleaded with him to *"come and see"* Jesus (John 1.46). Most scholars believe that the unnamed man with Andrew that first followed Jesus was John, son of Zebedee. That was Jesus' starting five. In just a few days Jesus had secured a handful of men who were curiously seeking him. Over the next eighteen months, Jesus would take these men on a roller coaster ride unlike anything they had ever experienced before. They followed him to a family wedding where Jesus performed his first miracle, transforming twenty large gallon jars of water into the best wine they had ever tasted (John 2.6-10). When these men saw this, they believed in Jesus (John 2.11). But they would see a lot more than that before too long! They followed Jesus to Jerusalem for the Passover and watched with shock as Jesus turned over the moneychanger's tables and confronted the Pharisees on their home turf (John 2.13-22). They marveled as Jesus spoke about being "born again" to Nicodemus, the religious leader. They listened to how God loved the world so much that he sent his only Son (John 3.3-16). They nervously followed Jesus into the forbidden territory of the Samaritans, and watched Jesus turn a casual conversation with a woman at a well into a life-altering encounter. As she ran back into the village she cried out, *"Come and see a man who told me all that I ever did. Can this be the Christ?"* (John 4.29). They watched as Jesus miraculously healed the son of a Roman noble official with a single word (John 4.50). They witnessed Jesus being rejected by his own hometown, refusing to believe that he was the Christ and even trying to take his life (Luke 4.28-30). For a year and a half these men saw Jesus open the door and say, "come and see" to just about every kind of person imaginable. Seekers and skeptics, religious elites and outcasts, the desperate and the hard-hearted. Jesus invited them all to "come and see"—to explore his claims and find answers to their spiritual questions.

The first step in any disciple-making strategy is the intentional engagement with people far from God, both religious and irreligious. It's not enough to just get the message of the gospel out, we must engage people in a way that they wrestle with the life and the claims of Jesus. I recently took my family on our summer vacation. Driving through a busy downtown area, we noticed men strategically positioned on street corners for several blocks. As we drew closer we could tell that these men were yelling out something as loudly as their voices would carry. As we got closer, I could tell they were screaming out scriptures and holding a Bible up in the air like an auctioneering ring man. Almost everyone who pulled up to the intersection rolled their windows up tightly and locked their doors. But it didn't seem to bother the preachers; they didn't even make eye contact. They just continued yelling out Bible verses. I'm sure those men had good intentions, but that is not how Jesus went about engaging people. He went where the people were. He engaged them in conversation. He addressed their specific needs, and at times even confronted their hard-heartedness. He gave them time to process what he was saying to them. His starting five men were in this phase for a year and a half. That's almost half of Jesus' total three-plus-year ministry! This was a critical time for these men. They were processing at high speed, trying to absorb all they were learning about Jesus. People reacted differently to Jesus. Some loved him, some hated him, some were drawn to him, and some were confused by him, but no one ignored him. Jesus made eye contact with everyone he met. For a church to be a disciple-making church, there must be intentional efforts to meet with people where they are and introduce them to Jesus.

## PHASE TWO: CONNECT BELIEVERS

The second phase in Jesus' disciple-making process was to call people to a commitment and connect them with other believers. After his rejection in Nazareth, Jesus relocated his ministry base of operation to Capernaum, a thriving city on the north shore of Galilee. During this time, John the Baptist was arrested by Herod Antipas. Jesus stepped into the vacuum of leadership and began preaching to the crowds that had been following John. Jesus also started preaching the simple message "repent and believe" (Matthew 4.12-17). It was also at this time that Jesus intentionally raised up a small group of emerging leaders. One day, Jesus walked along the shore of Galilee and saw Peter and Andrew tending to their fishing nets. He called out to them and said, *"Follow me and I will make you fishers of men."* These men dropped everything and followed Jesus. Then he walked down a bit further and saw James and John working with their father, Zebedee in the fishing boats and he called to them too, and they left it all to follow Jesus (Matthew 4.18-22). What's happening here is a big deal. Up to this point these men had been following Jesus, but they had not made a life-altering commitment to Jesus. They had observed him, listened to him, even marveled at him for the past year and a half, but they had not fully committed to him. Their lives had not been substantially altered, but that was about to change. Jesus called them to "follow him." This is what Dr. Wilkins describes as the "call of Jesus."

> "While the movement around him ebbed and flowed, Jesus' call established the high-tide mark for his form of discipleship. That call must be understood within the broader biblical concept of "calling" because it is a call that demands a decision of life commitment from those who are curious. The call focused people on making a commitment to Jesus, summoning them to place

their unreserved faith in him as the One coming with the proclamation of the kingdom. The call at this stage meant commitment to Jesus personally. It also included some sense of joining with Jesus in his announcement that the kingdom of God had arrived."[9]

When Jesus called these four men, he was asking them to make a commitment to him. He was asking them to leave what they had known before and follow him. He was asking them to trust him to provide for them, trust him to lead them, and trust him to use them for a greater purpose. He said, "follow me," and they followed him. From that point on, they were seen as Jesus' disciples. They publicly identified with Jesus. They lived in community with each other. They joined Jesus in his ministry. Over the next six months, they shadowed Jesus as he traveled, preached, and healed. Jesus was doing all the heavy lifting, but they were with him—helping him and watching him. They watched him cast a demon out of a man (Mark 1.21-28) and heal Peter's mother-in-law, as well as the thousands who flocked to Jesus for help (Luke 4.38-41). While fishing, they dropped their nets at Jesus' instruction and saw him orchestrate the largest catch of fish they had ever seen, proving that he was more than able to care for their needs (Luke 5.1-11). They saw Jesus heal lepers (Luke 5.12-16), forgive the paralytic (Luke 5.17-26), reach out to tax collectors (Luke 5.27-32), and wrangle with the religious legalists who loved external compliance with

---

9    *Following the Master*, pages 105-106.

the law more than people (Luke 5.33-39, 6.1-5). They also heard Jesus make bold declarations about himself, such as, *"The Father loves the Son and shows Him all things that He Himself is doing and greater works than these will He show Him, that you may marvel. For just as the Father raises the dead and gives them life, even so the Son also gives life to whom he wishes"* (John 5.20-21). And, *"Truly truly I say to you, he who hears my word and believes in him who sent me, has eternal life and will not come into judgment, but has passed out of death into life"* (John 5.24).

For a church to have a disciple-making strategy, they must not only share the gospel and help people find answers to their questions, but they must also call people to a commitment to follow Jesus. The curious cannot remain so forever. At some point, they must decide if Jesus is worth following or not. Those who do choose to follow Jesus must be connected to the community of believers. At our church, we talk about helping people make the four-point connection. Our goal is to help people that attend services on the weekend make four life-altering commitments. First, we want them to connect with Christ by placing their trust and faith in Jesus. Just as Jesus made his disciples "cross the line" of commitment, every week we encourage seekers to make a decision to follow Jesus. Second, we want new believers to connect with the church. Jesus called his disciples to publicly identify with him. This connection to the church happens through public baptism as well as attending our church membership seminar. Third, we want new believers to connect in a community. Jesus' disciples lived in community, and we want new believers in our church to do the same. This happens when they get plugged into a group where they can make lasting friendships, study the Bible, learn more about Jesus, and find the nurture and care they need. Fourth, we want new believers to connect with a cause. Jesus began to engage his men in ministry, even if it was at the entry level. We want to help people find some way to serve in the life of the church. It could be passing out coffee or greeting people as they enter the worship center. It could be expressing their gifts in other ways. But we want everyone to have a place to serve and a way to contribute to God's cause. We think of these four vital connections like four legs of a chair. If someone is balancing on one leg it is not very stable. Two legs are better, but still tenuous. Three legs (if that were possible) would be okay, but not as good as having all four legs squarely on the ground. The people who make all four commitments: to Christ, to the church, to a community, and to a cause are the people we say are fully connected and are ready to take the next step. Since it's our desire to move people from the crowd on Sunday into vital connection, we promote these four connection points strategically and frequently. We tell stories of people who made one of these commitments. We show video testimonies. We challenge people to take the next steps and celebrate them when they do. We try to remove the barriers that would keep people from making these commitments. We pray for God to move in their hearts.

Now, let me hit the pause button here. Most churches know that they need to be intentionally sharing the gospel with people far from God. For those who do come to Christ, they know they need to get them plugged into the church, into a group, and hopefully serving. But that's where they stop. For them, the win is getting people saved and in the church. It's icing on the cake if they serve and give, but there is no expectation for anything else. This is precisely where we are failing, because the next two steps in Jesus' strategy are the steps that move the church forward and cause it to grow! It would be like hitting a home run and racing past first base, tagging second base in full stride and then jogging to the dugout. These next two steps in Jesus' disciple-making strategy are crucial and transformational. So, let's keep going.

## PHASE THREE: GROW DISCIPLES

The third step in Jesus' disciple-making process was to train new believers to be and build disciples. At this point in Jesus' ministry, the crowds were swelling to uncontrollable numbers. Mark 3.7-8 says that a "great multitude" followed Jesus from Galilee, Judea, Jerusalem, and even from beyond the borders of Israel, like Tyre and Sidon. People desperate for healing were reaching out just to touch Jesus, and demons were shrieking out of the possessed at Jesus' command. Jesus knew that it was time to call his leadership team to a new level. He spent all night praying (Luke 6.12), and in the morning called twelve men to himself, appointing them as apostles. Mark clearly states why Jesus called these men. *"He appointed twelve (whom he also named apostles) so that they might be with him and he might send them out to preach...."* *(Mark 3.14).* This was Jesus' training program. Jesus Boot Camp. From this point forward, Jesus spent four times as much time with these twelve as he did with anyone else. They were clearly his top priority. Throughout the next six to nine months, Jesus poured into his disciples what it meant to be a part of the Kingdom of God. The more I study this period of time in Jesus' ministry, the more I become convinced that the kingdom of God was Jesus' main theme. It's as if teaching on the kingdom (the rule and reign of God on the earth and in heaven) was Jesus' curriculum for making disciples. Immediately after choosing his twelve leaders, Jesus sat them down and began to teach them about the Kingdom in what we know as the Sermon on the Mount. Jesus taught about the character of those in the kingdom of heaven (Matthew 5.1-12), the influence of those in the kingdom (Matthew 5.13-16), the morality of those in the kingdom (Matthew 5.17-48), and the spiritual practices of those in the kingdom (Matthew 6.1-24). He taught them about trust in the kingdom, forgiveness in the kingdom, and judgment in the kingdom (Matthew 6.25-7.27).

Following the sermon, Jesus demonstrated how a person enters the Kingdom of God. Those who exercise faith and trust in him, no matter their background, find acceptance in the kingdom. Those who reject Jesus, no matter their religious pedigree, fall short of the kingdom. Jesus marveled at the great faith of a Roman Centurion (Luke 7.1-10) and the humility of a sinful woman (Luke 7.36-50). Jesus also was grieved by the lack of faith of those in the Jewish communities of Chorazin and Bethsaida (Matthew 11.20-30) and the hard-hearted religious leaders who were always looking for a sign (Mark 3.20-30; Matthew 12.38-45). All the while, Jesus taught that those in the kingdom have a new family, the family of God (Luke 8.19-21).

During this time, Jesus taught about the kingdom of God using parables. Through stories about soils and seeds (Luke 8.5-18), wheat and tares (Matthew 13.24-30), leaven and bread (Matthew 13.33-35), treasures and pearls (Matthew 13.44-46), and fish and mustard seeds (Matthew 13.47-50; Mark 4.30-32) Jesus illustrated what the kingdom of heaven is like.

Jesus also demonstrated the power of the kingdom over earthly powers. He demonstrated his power over the natural elements by calming the storm (Luke 8.22-25). He demonstrated his power over demons by healing the demonic from Gerasene (Luke 8.26-39). He demonstrated his power over illness by healing a sick woman (Luke 8.43-48) and his power over death by raising a dead daughter (Luke 8.40-43, 49-56). Through it all, Jesus was preparing his disciples to do what he was doing. After approximately six to nine months, his disciples were ready to fly solo. He sent them out in pairs into the villages to preach repentance, and he gave them power over evil spirits (Matthew 11.1; Luke 9.6). When they came back, they reported all that had happened (Luke 9.10; Mark 6.30). He was intentionally training these men to reproduce.

For a church to be a disciple-making church, it must intentionally train people to walk with God and reproduce. When a soldier enlists in the Marines, he is immediately indoctrinated into that culture. The Marine Corps cuts the new recruits' hair, changes their clothes, and redefines their new family. Imagine what would happen if they did all of that and then simply released the new recruits to the front lines without training them to shoot a weapon or survive a firefight. They wouldn't last long. Unfortunately, that's what many churches do with new believers. We celebrate their new faith in Jesus, we accept them into the church, we give them a Bible, and teach them a few worship songs. But we never train them to walk with God on their own. We don't train them in the practical basics of prayer, Bible study, sharing their faith, forgiveness, love, and perseverance. We don't train them to rely on Jesus in a storm or to fight doubt and discouragement with truth. Is it any wonder that the attrition rate is so high in the church? Jesus intentionally trained his men, and we must do the same. In our church, we have chosen a few tools that we have used over the years to invest in the lives of people who are ready and wanting more. That training could last as long as nine months to a year. But the result is a disciple who is no longer dependent on someone else to feed him; he can feed himself. He is no longer an infant, but instead is a mature adult in the faith. He is mature, strong, tested, steady, and able to train others to be the same. The Apostle Paul said the purpose of the church is to train believers *"until we all attain to the unity of the faith and of the knowledge of the Son of God, to mature manhood to the measure of the stature of the fullness of Christ"* (Ephesians 4.13). He told the Colossians that his desire was to *"present everyone mature in Christ"* (Colossians 1.28). A disciple-making church trains, equips, and grows believers to be self-sustaining, reproducing followers of Christ.

## PHASE FOUR: GO MULTIPLY

Jesus' final phase in his disciple-making strategy was multiplication. At this point in Jesus' ministry, he pulled his disciples to a remote city in the far northern region of Israel on top of Mount Hermon, Caesarea Philippi. By this time things were heating up in Galilee. John the Baptist had been executed by Herod Antipas (Mark 6.17-29) and the people wanted to forcibly make Jesus their king (John 6.14-15). Add to that the fact that the same Herod who killed John the Baptist now had Jesus in his cross-hairs (Matthew 14.1-2). So Jesus took his men and retreated where they could pray. The region of Caesarea Philippi has a long history of pagan worship dating back to the days of Abraham. Even today, you can still see the remains of ancient ritual altars to Baal dating back thousands of years. In Jesus' day, the city was full of pagan worship, particularly the worship of Pan, a half-goat, half-man creature who promoted every kind of sexual deviancy. According to legend, he was so terrifying that still today we call his name when we say someone is *panicking*. There in the city, large temples were built in his honor, along with other pagan temples to Roman gods. The city was filled with idolatry and immorality. Also in the city was a large grotto from which came the rushing waters of Mount Hermon that feed the north Jordan River. Many believed that this grotto was the gateway to hades, the underworld. While Jesus was there with his disciples, he asked them a question. *"Who do the multitudes say that I am?"* The disciples gave Jesus the current popular opinion about him. "Some say you are John the Baptist, others think you are a prophet. Even some say you are Elijah." Then Jesus asked, "Who do you say that I am?" Peter boldly spoke up for the group, *"You are the Christ, the Son of the living God"* (Matthew 16.16). Jesus replied, *"Blessed are you, Simon Bar-Jonah! For flesh and blood has not revealed this to you, but my Father who is in heaven. And I tell you, you are Peter, and on this rock I will build my church, and the gates of hell shall not prevail against it"* (Matthew 16.17-18). Jesus was declaring that no matter what evil they see in the world, be it physical or spiritual, Herod or Pan, the church Jesus was establishing would always prevail. Today, you can go back and see the ruins of Pan—they are just a pile of rocks. You can go back and see the ancient ruins of Herod. But the church of Jesus Christ is alive and thriving!

But that church would not thrive without sacrifice. From this point, Jesus began to resolutely set his face toward Jerusalem (Luke 9.51) and the suffering he would endure on the cross. Three times, the death that awaited him in Jerusalem was accurately predicted (Luke 9.22, 43; 18.31). He called his men to be willing to suffer for the kingdom of God. He said, *"If anyone would come after me, let him deny himself and take up his cross daily and follow me. For whoever would save his life will lose it, but whoever loses his life for my sake will save it. For what does it profit a man if he gains the whole world and loses or forfeits himself? For whoever is ashamed of me and of my words, of him will the Son of Man be ashamed when he comes in his glory and the glory of the Father and of the holy angels"* (Luke 9.23-26). The kingdom of God would not advance without self-denial and sacrifice. On his way, a would-be disciple came to Jesus and said, "I will follow you wherever you go." Jesus told him plainly, "Foxes have holes, the birds of the air have nests, but the Son of Man has nowhere to lay his head." Another came and said, "I will follow you but let me bury my father first." Jesus replied, "Allow the dead to bury their own dead; but as far as you, go and proclaim everywhere the kingdom of God." Another said, "I will follow you, Lord but first permit me to say goodbye to those at home." Jesus flatly responded "No one, after putting his hand to plow and looking back, is fit for the kingdom of God" (Luke 9.57-62). Jesus was calling for sacrifice. On another occasion Jesus taught about the cost of discipleship. *"If anyone comes to Me, and does not hate his own father and mother and wife and children and brothers and sisters, yes and even his own life he cannot be my disciple. Whoever does not carry his own cross and come after Me cannot be my disciple...So therefore, no one of you can be My disciple who does not give up all his own possessions"* (Luke 14.26-27,33). Before long, Jesus appointed seventy-two other disciples to go and preach in advance of his coming in the regions of Perea (Transjordan) and Judea. The twelve had now multiplied to seventy-two. When they returned to report all that God had done through them, Jesus was filled with joy (Luke 10.21). This is the only place in scripture where we see that Jesus was filled with joy. What brought Jesus such exuberant joy? It was seeing the men he had trained, multiplying and preaching the gospel. He was seeing multiplication to the fourth generation. He was seeing the igniting of a movement!

As the days drew closer for Jesus to head to the cross, he warned his disciples. He warned them against hypocrisy (Luke 12.1-12). He warned them against greed (Luke 12.13-34). He warned them against pride (Mark 10.35-45). He warned them again being unprepared for his second coming (Luke 12.35-48). He warned them about division and conflict (Luke 12.49-59). Jesus also taught them about persistence in prayer (Luke 18.1-14) and the assurance of his return (Luke 17.22-37). On the night before he was betrayed, Jesus prayed for his disciples. He prayed to his Father, *"I glorified you on earth, having accomplished the work that you gave me to do"* (John 17.4). Jesus had accomplished his work. No, he had not gone to the cross yet. That wasn't the work he was referring to here. Jesus had accomplished the work of calling out disciples who were trained and prepared to multiply a movement.

If a church is going to be a disciple-making church, it must have a plan for multiplication. You must be able to train up men and women who not only know how to walk with God, but can also train others to do the same. This kind of multiplication only comes at a high cost. It requires sacrifice. It requires self-denial. It may even require suffering. But men and women who know Jesus and are committed to multiplication at any cost are simply unstoppable. The early church rapidly multiplied because the disciples had been trained by Jesus to do just that (Acts 6.7).

As you look at your church, do you see people moving through these four phases of ministry? Do you see people exploring the claims of Christ and engaging with believers to find answers to spiritual questions? Do you see new believers coming to Christ, being baptized, joining the church, getting plugged into a group or Bible study and beginning to serve? Do you see growing believers being intentionally trained to be disciples and build disciple makers? Do you see those trained up believers now multiplying the ministry by leading people to Christ, investing in new believers, or leading out in new areas of growth and outreach? This is what a church looks like that follows Jesus' plan of making disciples. You could summarize Jesus' four-phased process like this: **Engage Explorers, Connect Believers, Grow Workers, and Go Multiply**.

## JESUS OR APPLE

Not long ago I was in the Apple store working on my iPhone. A young lady was helping me—she probably looked to be in her early twenties. While she was working on my phone I starting talking to her about her job. I asked, "Have you been working here long?" "No, not really. Just a few months," she said. "Do you like working here?" Her face lit up, "Oh yes!" Seeing her enthusiasm, I decided to inquire further. "Well, I bet it's hard, learning all this stuff. You must have had to sit through hours and hours of training, right?" She smiled. "Not really." I asked, "So how did you learn to do what you do?" She said, "Well, I went online and saw there were job openings, so I registered for a two-day seminar hosted at a local hotel ball room. After two days, they placed me in a store and assigned me to a mentor. For the first few weeks I just wore regular clothes and the mentor wore the bright Apple shirt and lanyard. I just watched everything he did and took it all in. After dealing with a customer, he would ask me if I had questions or we would discuss that particular situation." By this time she had stopped working on my phone and was completely into this story, so I kept listening. "Then," she said, "after a while, I put on the Apple shirt and lanyard and my mentor dressed in regular clothes and he followed me around as I took care of customers.

If I had a problem, he was ready to jump in and help. When he thought I was ready, he just set me free to go on my own. Now I'm prepared to do the same things with another trainee!" She smiled. I did, too. Because what she described was disciple making, Jesus style. Jesus took in curious men, drew them to faith, let them shadow him for a season, and then he cut them loose to go on their own. When they were ready, he watched them reproduce into seventy-two more men. His plan was so simple and yet so profound. Jesus drew men to himself, let them follow him until they got it, and then he sent them out to reproduce. When I look at the modern church, I'm grieved that somehow along the way we've missed the strategy of Jesus. Somehow we traded making disciples for making decisions. Somehow we traded a clear process with running programs. We stopped moving people through stages of maturity and started shuffling people between services. Somehow along the way we thought that if we got people to worship and in a group that they would figure it all out and become strong, when in fact, the church has become weak. We've forgotten that the church exists to train up men and women who will take the gospel to their offices and neighborhoods and the world, and we started just trying to fill seats. What Jesus gave us was simple, reproducible, and powerful. Apple gets it. Do you?

**Men** and **women** who **know Jesus** and are committed to **multiplication** at any cost **are** simply **unstoppable**.

**Ministry** in the early church was a **high-touch**, relationally-intensive, **people-driven ministry**."

# 4

# MOVE FROM RELIGIOUS ACTIVITY TO RELATIONAL INVESTMENT

"So if I buy in to what you are saying, what is going to be different about my ministry six months from now?" It was a good question, coming from a seasoned pastor. As we shared lunch together in a nice restaurant, the topic of conversation was making disciples. This pastor had led his church to become one of the most influential churches in his district, seeing people come to Christ and watching the church expand. However, over the past few years the church numbers were beginning to sag. Other churches in the area were gaining traction while his ministry was sputtering. He wanted to know more about making disciples because God had put in his heart that the problem was deeper than just the weekend attendance.

He was convinced that he needed to raise up stronger, more committed believers, but he was unclear what that would look like or how to do it. Around that table we talked about Jesus as the model for making disciples and the definition of a disciple. I briefly explained that Jesus had a simple four-step strategy for producing disciples and disciple makers. Then he dropped the question. "What's going to be different six months from now if I course-correct and head this direction?" You may be wondering the same thing. Up until now, you probably agree with most of what you've read. But does disciple making really make a difference in a church? The short answer is yes. Disciple making changes the DNA of your church from being about managing activities to investing in people.

## LIFE ON LIFE

People matter to God. Christ died for people. Ministry in the early church was a high-touch, relationally-intensive, people-driven ministry. They were devoted to one another. They cared for each another, sharing their resources and time together and encouraging each other. Think about it. When the Apostle Paul wrote his letters, he never mentioned activities; he talked about people. He wrote to people that he loved and addressed their fears and problems. He invested in people with his time and effort and energy. The church at Thessalonica was a church that Paul planted on his second missionary journey. He entered the city and immediately began preaching about

Jesus in the synagogue with great success. Many people believed the gospel, including Jews and many devout Greeks. They formed a church that met in Jason's house (Acts 17.1-9). But the Jews in the city became jealous of Paul and created a riot. Dragging Jason before the city authorities, they said, *"These men who have turned the world upside down have come here also..."* (Acts 17.6). Although Paul and Silas had to leave the city, God was mightily at work and the church began to grow, making disciples and sharing the gospel. Paul later wrote a letter to this church he loved.

> "For we know, brothers loved by God, that he has chosen you, because our gospel came to you not only in word, but also in power and in the Holy Spirit and with full conviction. You know what kind of men we proved to be among you for your sake. And you became imitators of us and of the Lord, for you received the word in much affliction, with the joy of the Holy Spirit, so that you became an example to all the believers in Macedonia and in Achaia. For not only has the word of the Lord sounded forth from you in Macedonia and Achaia, but your faith in God has gone forth everywhere."
> I Thessalonians 1.4-8

This tiny house church that started in the furnace of controversy had grown to be one of the most influential churches in the region. Notice, though, as you read this letter that Paul wrote to that church, he doesn't discuss ministry strategy or new growth initiatives. He writes about his love for them. *"We were gentle among you, like a nursing mother taking care of her own children. So, being affectionately desirous of you, we were ready to share with you not only the gospel of God but also our own selves because you had become very dear to us"* (I Thessalonians 2.7-8). Paul is saying, "We loved you like crazy and when we came to you, we were protective of you, like a young mom nursing and caring for her children. And we didn't just come to you with the message of the gospel, we gave our whole selves to you because we loved you so much." Can you feel how much Paul loved them? He keeps going. *"For you know how, like a father with his children, we exhorted each one of you and encouraged you and charged you to walk in a manner worthy of God, who calls you into his own kingdom"* (I Thessalonians 2.11-12). He said, "Not only were we like a nurturing mother to you, we were also like a loving father to you. We instructed you, taught you, modeled the life of Christ before you and challenged you to live your life for God and his kingdom." Nurture and discipline. Care and challenge. Paul invested his life and his heart heavily in these people, and over time his love for them had not diminished. *"But since we were torn away from you, brothers, for a short time, in person not in heart, we endeavored the more eagerly and with great desire to see you face to face, because we wanted to come to you—I, Paul, again and again—but Satan hindered us"* (I Thessalonians 2.17-18). Can you hear the longing in his heart to be with these people? He talks like a parent that has been torn from his children and his heart breaks because he can't be with them. I remember the day Liz and I took our oldest daughter off to college for the first time. We moved her stuff into the dorm room and spent the day decorating and shopping. Then the time came when we had to say goodbye. The drive home was long and hard. There were lots of tears cried that night. Over the next several weeks, I couldn't wait until I could see her again. I was constantly thinking about her. How is she doing? Are things ok? Is she making it without us? When can I see her next? That's what I hear when I read Paul's letter. These people were on his heart and on his mind and he couldn't wait to see them again. Then he writes these powerful words. *"For what is our hope and joy or crown of boasting before our Lord Jesus at his coming? Is it not you? For you are our glory and joy"* (I Thessalonians 2.19-20). Did you get that? Paul said that when he stands before Christ one day, his hope and joy and reward for ministry is simply going to be the fact that they are in heaven with him. Them in heaven will make all his efforts and struggles worth it. Let me ask you a really important question. Do you love your people like that? Are you nurturing them like a mother and challenging them like a father? Are you brokenhearted when you are away from them and all the while you are thinking and praying for them? Is your joy and hope and reward tied up in the lives of people you are loving and leading? For many pastors, the answer to these questions is simply...no. When the pastor becomes a disconnected leader of programs and initiatives without any real personal investment in the people he is leading, ministry becomes a frustration. When the people don't think that their pastor really knows them or loves them, they aren't open to hearing what he has to say about anything. In all the deluge of material on leadership and church growth, we must never forget that our job is to invest our lives in people. That's how Paul did it. And that is how Jesus did it.

On the night before his death, Jesus was reflecting on the three plus years he had invested in his men. He had plucked them out of virtual obscurity; tax collectors, fishermen, political zealots, and businessmen. Over that time he had poured his life into them. He loved them. He challenged them. He rebuked them and pushed them. He encouraged them and protected them. And now he was about to leave them. John 13.1 says, *"Now before the Feast of the Passover, when Jesus knew that his hour had come to depart out of this world to the Father, having loved his own who were in the world, he loved them to the end."* Jesus loved them. He loved them enough to invest his life in them. He loved them enough to wash their feet that night. And he loved them enough to endure the cross. I'm convinced that there is a direct relationship between love and investment. If a pastor invests little, he loves little. If a pastor pours his life into the people in his church: training, investing, encouraging, and challenging them, then his love for them will be huge. I remember a seasoned pastor told me one time when I was just getting into the ministry, "Son, always keep the desk between you and the people." I thought it was bad advice then, and I know it is horrible advice now. Jesus didn't do ministry that way. Paul didn't do ministry that way. Can you be hurt if you put your heart out there? Yes. Will you be let down and disappointed? Yes. But if you don't, you will eventually lose the joy in ministry altogether. The joy in ministry is found in your personal investment in the lives of people and in watching them invest in others to the glory of God! That's what keeps you going in ministry over the long haul. When I look back over my twenty years of ministry, what brings me the most joy is not a great series I preached or a record attendance on a weekend. What brings me joy today are the faces of men that I have personally discipled and invested my life in who are still walking with God and investing their lives in other men. As I'm writing this chapter, I received a text from one of my dear friends, Greg. Greg played football for Texas A&M back in the eighties as a nose guard. His nick name was "Bone Crusher" because of the violent way he tackled running backs. When he and his wife, Tina joined our church, we hit it off immediately. His fun personality and winsome smile attracted people easily. Greg was also an incredible singer and had come from a mega church in Houston where he was on the worship team. He and his family plugged right in and started serving in various ways. One day I invited Greg to lunch and talked to him about Jesus' plan for making disciples. The thought of someone personally investing in his life touched him in a profound way. He had never had anyone really take a spiritual interest in him before. We started to meet together. We memorized scripture. We talked about Jesus' plan for making disciples. At the end of five weeks, we had completed a small workbook together, and I told Greg that I was cutting him loose to invest in another man. When he had reproduced what I had already shown him, then we would get back together. That was like saying, "sick 'em" to a dog! Greg found a few men and started doing what I had shown him. Along the way I kept up with how he was doing and debriefed issues he was facing. Once he had reproduced, we celebrated together and I began to invest more time in him. We went through another book that takes about four months to complete. It was in that season of time that God revealed some things to Greg about his grace and forgiveness that were completely overwhelming. Greg was not the same man he used to be. He was a new creation in Christ. God was setting his heart on fire to invest in men. Even when Greg faced a job change and was forced to start his own business, he was settled in the Lord, confident that God was working all this together for his good. He would tell me about sharing the gospel with guys on the job site. We laughed a lot. Cried sometimes. Once we had completed the book, I sent Greg out to reproduce, and he did once again. Somehow he always found men to invest in. Men who were sitting in church, going through programs, but not being challenged to really walk with Jesus. Greg and I would continue to meet over the next year as he and I both discipled men. We shared both the joys and disappointments. We were in the trenches together, shoulder to shoulder, doing the work. One afternoon I was attending a parent gathering at my oldest daughter's university. A nice young couple sat at our table. The man leaned over and said, "I think I know you. Are you Craig from Colleyville?" "Yes, I am," I replied. He said, "Do you know Greg?" "Oh yes! We are good friends! How do you know him?" He said, "Greg discipled me just like you discipled him!" Then he said with a smile, "I guess that makes me your grandson!" We all got a big laugh, but inside, my heart was full. Recently Greg moved out of state to work for a new company. He just sent me a picture of a memory verse we used to quote to one another with the text, "Thinking about you...thanks brother." I know that God is going to use Greg where he has planted him. He already has a man lined up to start meeting with. But I'm telling you, there is no joy like the joy of investing your life in people.

## BREAKING THROUGH EXCUSES

When I talk to leaders about personally investing in people, I often get a bit of push back. For some reason there is a resistance when it comes to personal investment in people. When I first became a pastor, I didn't know much about how to invest in a man's life. Most of my training had been in the Seminary classroom and in the management of programs in a large suburban church. But there were three businessmen who caught my attention.

They were all three very successful in their careers. One owned his own construction business, another was a macular facial surgeon, and the third managed and sold real estate. All of these men were extremely busy, juggling high commitments and loaded schedules, but all three were committed to discipling men. I saw them get up early in the morning to meet with a man before breakfast. I saw them stay up late at night to disciple a group of men. I saw them go to a man's office and disciple him there. They all used different tools and methods, but they were committed to personal investment. That was something I had never seen from any pastor I had served under. I had never even experienced it as a church member before God called me into vocational ministry, but I was seeing it now lived out in three businessmen. One of these men would often challenge me, "Ask God to give you a man, and then invest in him until he's ready to do the same with another man." It seemed so simple, how could I have missed it? The Apostle Paul put it this way: *"And what you have heard from me in the presence of many witnesses entrust to faithful men who will be able to teach others also"* (2 Timothy 2.2). In this one verse, Paul refers to four generations of disciples: Paul, Timothy, faithful men, and others. Any time a man can invest his life in a man who will in turn do the same to the fourth generation, God will use him to ignite a movement. That's God's plan for every one of us – to be movement catalysts who make disciples and produce disciple makers. But why are so many pastors reluctant to make the personal investment? Here are some of the most common excuses. **I don't have time.** This is by far the most common excuse. "You don't understand my crazy schedule. I've got sermons to prepare, meetings to attend, counseling to do, hospital visits to make, staff to manage, visitors to follow up, problems to solve, budgets to review...I just can't add one more thing to my pile." I get it. Pastors are busy. I am one. I know what it is like to work from before sunrise to after sunset and still not get everything done. I know what it is like to have the deadline of Sunday breathing down your neck and the people expecting your sermon to be fresh, creative, and wonderful. I know that there are lots of people who need help and lots of hurting people who need your attention. I get it. But one of the perks of being a pastor is you determine your schedule. You decide what's top priority. When I first started transitioning a church to become a disciple-making church, I had to come to the realization that most of what I was doing was good, but not much of it was moving the church forward. I was managing programs, launching initiatives, overseeing budgets and staff, but I wasn't investing my life in anyone and I was losing the joy of serving. I determined that if personal investment was Jesus' top priority, it should be mine, too. I began to shift my schedule and create space for me to start investing in men. Listen, everyone is busy. Most of the men you will disciple are busy, too. If you expect them to carve out time away from their careers and family to invest in men, then you need to lead the way by showing how it can be done, even in a busy schedule. Busy-ness isn't a reason to not make disciples, it's an excuse. And a poor one at that. I can just imagine you standing before Jesus one day, at the Judgment Seat of Christ (2 Corinthians 5.10) where your life and ministry will be evaluated, saying, "Jesus, I would have done what you said, but I was so busy." Something tells me Jesus isn't going to be satisfied with that answer. If he's not going to be satisfied with it then, he's not satisfied with it now.

**I've never been discipled before.** I'm a bit more sympathetic to this excuse because the unfortunate realization is that most pastors don't disciple men because they have never been discipled themselves. Most have grown up in low-investment/highly programmed churches, led by low-investment/highly programmed pastors. Programs and production get celebrated. Life investment gets ignored. It is important, but not urgent, therefore it never gets done. Let me ask you, are you going to let the failures of others be your excuse for failing to do the one thing Jesus commanded you to do? While you may have never been discipled by another person, you know more about how to follow Jesus and share your faith than 99.9% of the people in your congregation. Plus, you have the Spirit of God in you. You are more than qualified to invest in another man. When I got started, I hadn't been formally discipled. But when I look back over my life, I see that God had put people in my life that influenced me toward Jesus in powerful ways. My guess is that you have people like that, too–people God used to build you up and help you walk with Him. So, while you may not have been formally discipled, you are prepared and competent to invest in others. This is why making disciples requires great faith! Hebrews 11.6 says, "Without faith it is impossible to please God." The essence of faith is trusting God to act according to His promises. So think about it this way, if Jesus commanded you to go make disciples, and if he promised that he would be with you "even to the end of the age" (Matthew 28.20), then don't you think you can trust him to work through you? You can let excuses hold you back or you can take a leap of faith and trust God to work through you to impact the life of another person. Trust God. And if you feel incompetent or unsure of how to invest in another person, then find someone experienced and let them be a coach for you. Look around for people who are passionate about making disciples and ask if you can meet with them. Ask questions. Get tips and insights. Find solutions to problems. Read great books and blogs. Go to conferences. The resources are available and the Spirit is ready. God will use you powerfully if you just take a step of faith. He can do more through you than you think He can!

**I invest in people through my preaching and counseling.** Some pastors tell me that they don't need to disciple anyone personally because they do that every week through their preaching and counseling ministry. While preaching and counseling are vitally important to a disciple-making church, they cannot replace the one on one, or small group training in a disciple-making relationship. Preaching is unilateral; I speak...you listen. Disciple making is back and forth conversation. Preaching is information; disciple making is about life transformation. Preaching is about content; disciple making is about character. Preaching happens in the building; disciple making happens outside the building. Preaching tells a man what to do; disciple making shows a man what to do. Preaching is in-the-pew training; disciple making is on-the-job training. In preaching, you are accountable to deliver God's Word; in disciple making the other person is accountable to obey God's Word. Preaching educates leaders; disciple making equips leaders. Preaching can't be reproduced; disciple making is intended to be reproduced. There is a big difference between preaching and disciple making. Both are needed. Jesus did both very well. However, Jesus spent four times as much time discipling his men as he did preaching to the crowds. Four to one. That shows you the importance of disciple making in the life of Jesus.

**It's not my personality or passion.** Some leaders just dismiss disciple making because it's not what they like to do or not what they feel wired to do. Some guys are just introverts and really don't like to be around people. Other guys are more passionate about preaching, leading, vision casting, counseling, or personal evangelism. But just because you don't think disciple making fits your personality or passion doesn't excuse you from faithfully discharging the ministry God has placed in your hands to make disciples. Paul told Timothy, *"Preach the word, be ready in season and out of season; reprove, rebuke, and exhort with complete patience and teaching...be sober minded, endure suffering, do the work of an evangelist, fulfill your ministry"* (2 Timothy 4.2, 5). Most pastors read "preach the word" and stop there, envisioning great sermons flowing out of their pulpits with people hanging on their every word. Certainly we are called to preach God's Word faithfully. But Paul goes on to say that we are to "reprove, rebuke, exhort" with all the patience the Spirit can give us. That doesn't just happen in a one-way preaching context, that happens after the preaching is over and you are face to face with people. The best place for reproving and rebuking is in the context of a disciple-making relationship when you have their heart and their trust. Paul closes with a charge to *"fulfill your ministry."* Jesus clearly told us our ministry objective...make disciples of all nations. So a failure to invest in people and train them to do the same would be a failure to fulfill the ministry given to you by Christ.

**I can't show favoritism by just focusing on a few people.** Many pastors feel like there is no way they could invest in a few men because other men in the church would become jealous or resentful. It simply would not be politically wise to show preference to one certain group. I realize that this may be more of an issue in some churches than in others. Some cultures are supersensitive to the pastor's actions and pick up any whiff of preferential treatment. But again, Jesus didn't let that hold him back.

Jesus clearly identified leaders (Matthew 4.18-19), and those leaders were the ones in which he invested his life. Almost every church recognizes existing leaders and emerging leaders. That is often the best place to start. If a man is a recognized leader in the church, then people would expect the Pastor to be meeting with him. So start with your leaders. If you have church staff, start with your staff. Then help those leaders to begin reproducing. Another benefit to starting with existing leaders is that you will have their influence and support when you later branch out to discipling new and emerging leaders.

**I am afraid to show people who I really am.** I believe this excuse is very real and very personal. There are many church leaders who agree that we should be personally investing time in others, but somehow find ways not to do it. Digging deeper, the fear of self-disclosure is the real culprit. To invest in another person means that I must take my mask off and reveal myself, problems and all. It means I must live an authentic life. It means that people will see in me a true love for God, passion for the Word, and concern for those far from God, or the lack thereof. This is why many feel much more comfortable running programs and managing ministries, because they can do that and never get too close to anyone. They can be busy, but not lay their hearts bare. They can be seen as good pastors or leaders without feeling vulnerable or exposed. To those of you who honestly struggle in this area, I want to encourage you. Hear my heart. People will never open their hearts to you until you open your heart to them. Is it risky? Sure it is. Jesus held nothing back and he was hurt for a time. Paul opened his heart and felt the sting of rejection and disappointment. But you will never know the joy and impact of ministry by keeping people at arm's length. Open your heart. Live your life in authenticity. Love those in your life with a deep love. Be honest with yourself and with those in whom you are investing your life. Give of yourself freely just as Christ has given himself freely to you. To this you were called.

**I need something that will produce fast results.** This is often an unspoken excuse, but it is real. Most of the time, pastors are not even thinking about disciple making until something has gone wrong in their church. If the numbers are up and the church is growing, there is little thought to making disciples. "Things are obviously working great," they say, "so why change it?" But when the downturn comes, then pastors are open to a change of course. Unfortunately, many times what they are looking for is a quick fix to a deep problem. "Just give me another program or sermon series that will draw the people and I'm good," they say. But making disciples isn't a quick fix, it's a life decision. It is something you do because you are convinced that Jesus made disciples and you are committed to walk as Jesus walked (I John 2.6).

The church doesn't need men of excuses, it needs men of action. Men who will follow the example of Jesus and the Apostle Paul. Men who will love the people in their church enough to step down off the platform and into their lives and show them how to walk with Christ.

Jesus' method for making disciples was grounded in relationships. Making disciples requires you to build relationships with the people in your church in a way that motivates them toward Christ-likeness. Simply put, you can't microwave life change. You can't assembly line personal transformation. People don't change by simply dropping them on a church conveyor belt and running them through various programs and activities. Life change happens one person at a time. One life at a time.

## DON'TS AND DOS

Before you dive into making disciples in your church, let me encourage you with a few Dos and Don'ts. Often pastors, in their zeal to make disciples, inadvertently do things that actually make it harder for them to do so effectively. So here are some practical warnings.

**Don't start casting vision about disciple making immediately. Do start making disciples immediately.** Probably the biggest mistake pastors make in disciple making is they reveal their vision and passion for making disciples too quickly and then turn it into a church program that usually has a short shelf life. There will be a time for vision casting and preaching on disciple making, but not at the very beginning. Instead, keep vision casting one on one. Look for a man to disciple and start investing in his life. Help him to reproduce and do the same. Work under the radar. That is what Jesus did. For the first year and half, Jesus didn't preach to massive crowds, casting his vision of disciple making. Initially John the Baptist drew the crowds, Jesus was content to work in the shadows. He worked under the radar of John's public ministry, quietly investing in five men. When the time came for him to go public, he already had men ready to begin reproducing. Jesus said the Kingdom of God is like a bit of leaven that silently and invisibly works through the whole dough (Matthew 13.33). So don't begin from the pulpit, begin at the coffee shop. Start quietly investing in men. You may ask, "Why is this important?" First, it allows you to field-test your methods to discover what works best for you. You don't want to take something church wide that won't work in your context. Second, it allows you to build a tribe of supporters. Once you go public with your vision of disciple making, you will have people who can attest to the power of it and how their lives have been changed. Any naysayers will be outnumbered. Third, once you begin to publicly speak about disciple making, people will want to be discipled. If you start quietly making disciples first, when the demand is there, you will have people ready to meet that demand and disciple the people in your church.

**Don't turn disciple-making over to another staff person. Do lead the charge yourself.** The quickest way to kill a disciple making movement in your church is to relegate it to another staff member while you fail to get involved. Remember, disciple making is 90% modeling what the Christian life looks like to other men. You must set the pace yourself. Your actions speak louder than your words. I know many pastors who can preach heartfelt, amazing sermons on discipleship. I know pastors who have written powerful best-selling books on discipleship. But the problem is, they don't do it. The minute people hear you saying one thing but see you doing another, you lose their heart and their trust. Pastor, hear me. You must give yourself to investing in the men in your church. Make disciples. Live authentically before them. Give them an example to follow. Walk with God on your own and share what God is speaking to you. Build relationships with men who don't know Christ and regularly share the gospel with them. Have a few men you are investing in on a regular basis. When the men in your church start seeing you do these things, they will follow you! Don't turn this into a program that will eventually die. Don't give this responsibility over to someone else. You set the pace and model for your men what it means to know Christ and invest in others. If you will lead by example, they will follow you anywhere.

**Don't do a mass sign up. Do select the people yourself.** Some pastors want to preach on discipleship and then say, "If you want to be discipled, sign up at the info desk." This way he makes the appeal to everyone. But this strategy has some problems. First, that is not how Jesus did it. When it came to training men, Jesus always took the initiative (Matthew 4.18-19). Mark 3.13 reports that Jesus "*called to him those whom he desired.*" Jesus picked the guys he wanted to spend time with. Jesus always looked for the men who were spiritually curious. The first men Jesus discipled were men who came after Jesus with spiritual questions (John 1.39). I have found that the best person to disciple is not the man who thinks he already knows everything. It's the man who is hungry, eager, and ready to learn. That is the kind of person you want to disciple. Second, if you get one hundred people wanting to be discipled, there is no way you can personally do everyone yourself. Unless you have prepared a group first, that plan is going to fail fast. Third, you want to be sure that the people you initially invest in have the capability of reproducing. Not everyone is ready for this phase. You wouldn't want to invest a large amount of your time in a person who will never take what you have shown them and invest in others. Better to do what Jesus did, select the ones that are ready and that will be most productive.

**Don't underestimate the power of a few men who walk with God. Do prioritize reaching and training men.** The story is often told about when Dawson Trotman, the founder of The Navigators, was recruiting counselors for one of Billy Graham's Crusades in a large city. He called supporting churches asking them for help. He asked one secretary who answered the phone if they had many men or women in their church who knew their Bibles well and could lead someone to Christ. She replied, "Would you repeat the qualifications again, please?" So Dawson did. After a long pause, the secretary replied, "You know we did have a man like that in our church once, but he moved away."[10] Unfortunately, I'm sure that church is not the exception. Does your church have a list of men who

---

10    *The Lost Art of Making Disciples*, LeRoy Eims, page 61.

know their Bibles and can lead someone to Christ? A list of men who are trained, proven, solid, and ready at a moment's call? There is a crying need for men like this. Think about it. If a man is walking with God, chances are good he will lead his wife and children to walk with God. Reach the man, reach the family. The man will provide spiritual leadership in his home, at his office, and in the church. For generations, God has used godly women to give leadership to the church. If it weren't for godly women, like those who invested in young Timothy's life (2 Timothy 1.5) the church would not be as strong as it is today. However, over time men have taken a back seat in spiritual leadership both in the home and at the church. A 2002 Gallup poll revealed, *"A mountain of Gallup survey data attests to the idea that women are more religious than men, hold their beliefs more firmly, practice their faith more consistently, and work more vigorously for the congregation."*[11] Today, the typical church in America draws a crowd that is 61% female and 39% male. On any given Sunday in America, there are 13 million more women than men in church.[12] But when pastors and leaders begin to invest in men, then men begin to step into the roles of leadership they have long since abandoned.

When God gets ahold of man's heart, there is a generational impact. That's why the last prophecy in the Old Testament is a promise that before the Lord comes, he will *"turn the hearts of fathers to their children and*

---

11      Gallup.com George Gallup Jr, *Why are Women More Religious?* December 17, 2002.
12      Church for men.com quick facts on the gender gap.

*the hearts of children to their fathers"* (Malachi 4.6). Don't underestimate the power of godly men.

# FIRST STEPS

Now that you are ready to get started, let me give you some practical "how-to's" for investing in men.

**Select the right person.** When you begin to make disciples in your church, beginning with the right person is critical. I can remember when I was a new pastor and God was burdening me about making disciples. I remember one of the businessmen who invested in me saying, "Craig, just pray for God to give you one man to pour your life into." So, I started praying. After a few days, a young man walked into our church whom I had never met before. He was in his early twenties, stocky athletic build with short hair, and fresh out of college. I introduced myself to him. "Hey, my name is Gibson," he relied. He just felt impressed to come to our church that day and check it out. Immediately I felt the Spirit prompt me. "You prayed for a guy. Well, here he is." That next week, I invited Gibson out to eat and I asked him if he would be interested in meeting together for some time to grow in his relationship with Christ. He said he would love to. In the meantime, God brought two other college grads across my path. The four of us started meeting early in the morning. We studied God's word, memorized scripture, prayed together, and talked openly about struggles. I walked them through a study that they could use to reproduce with other people. As I look back on that season, God did a great work in the lives of those men. Today, each one is married and has a family of his own. Two men work in Christian schools, one as a principal and the other as a coach. They are faithfully investing their lives in men and students. Gibson graduated from Seminary, got married to a girl on our church staff, has four children, and is planting a church in Philadelphia. He still hasn't lost the fire to make disciples. In fact, just a few months ago Gibson told me his side of the story. He had been praying for God to bring a man into his life to show him how to grow spiritually. As he was driving down the street of our church, the Spirit of God quickly prompted him to pull into the parking lot. He said, "I had never been in that church before, but God told me to pull in that night." That was the night we met. Here is what I know...God sees the big picture, and He is always willing and ready to bring a faithful disciple across the path of an open seeker. If you are asking him to lead you, then He will lead you to the person you are to pour your life into.

Here are some things to look for when you select a person to disciple. First, start with your existing leaders. As I've said before, the people in the church expect you to spend time with existing leaders. So, start there. Are there any existing leaders who would be open and hungry to be trained to walk with God? If so, then begin with them. When I came to Colleyville, I started with our Leadership Team and worked from there. If they are already in leadership, I certainly want them walking with Jesus. So look first to your leaders. Second, look for people who are hungry for more. We call them "poppers." These are people who pop up out of the crowd. They are always there. They are eager to learn. They have spiritual questions. They are growing and you sense a teachable attitude. Paul told Timothy to select "faithful men" who had the capacity to teach others (2 Timothy 2.2). I've always heard the acrostic F.A.T.—faithful, available, and teachable. Third, start with already seasoned believers. This may sound a bit counterintuitive. You would think to start with a new believer who doesn't know much and really needs it. But in the beginning you want to start with people who are solid and could rapidly reproduce. Soon you will have an army of people who can come alongside new believers. Fourth, follow the prompting of the Spirit. As you start looking for men to train, the Spirit will lead you to the right person, just as he led me to Gibson.

**Pick a tool.** Every carpenter has a hammer. Every surgeon has a scalpel. Every mechanic has a wrench. And every disciple maker has a tool that they use to invest in others. When I say a tool, I mean some kind of material that intentionally trains the person being discipled in the skills you think they need to know. Remember, this training is to instill in new believers the character and competencies of Jesus, so pick a tool that accomplishes that and use it. Now some people have said, "The Bible is my tool." And that sounds really good. The only problem with that is when you get three to four generations deep, there is no way to know if what you trained your guy to do is going to be what is reproduced down the line. Tools help ensure that the investment you make is easily reproducible. All the great disciple-making ministries (Navigators, Campus Crusade, CBMC) have tools they have created and that they use consistently over time. You may want to create your own, but you certainly don't have to. There are many materials available today that you can choose from that will work just fine. My suggestion is to look around and find the tool you are most comfortable with and start using it. You might even want to test drive a few to see how you like them, but find a tool and stick with it. At our church we utilize many of the tools written by Navigators. We also use a tool called "One on One with God" that was written by Jerry Fine, one of the men who discipled me in Oklahoma City. These are tools we have used and we know are easily reproduced. As you find a tool that works best for you, over time you will see people reproducing it to the third and fourth generation! Now, let me add a warning here. The tool in no way replaces the person. You can get someone through material. But life change happens when they see your life and your example. Tools are helpful for reproduction. But the power of disciple making comes in your personal investment.

**Guard your time.** This is, of course, one of the biggest issues for pastors. There is so much to do and so little time to do it. Often personal investment in people gets pushed to the side for more urgent matters. But I have found that if I schedule something, I can protect it. For years my wife and I have had planning date nights. We will go on a date, maybe a nice dinner or out for coffee.

Then we will open up both of our calendars (or pull them up on our phones) and we will schedule our lives for the next four to six months. We will put down all the school dates and kids' activities. We'll input all the key events at church. Then we will schedule our date nights. We go out on a date at least once every two weeks. When we were younger with no kids we went on a date once a week. But with our hectic pace, once every two weeks works perfectly. Now we do this for one reason. If we don't schedule our date nights well in advance, they don't happen. The busy-ness of life crowds out what's most important—our marriage. The same is true with disciple making. Dr. Stephen Covey has a matrix familiar to most business leaders. On the X axis is urgency, and on the Y axis is importance. The top left quadrant is very important but not urgent. The top right quadrant is very important and very urgent. The bottom left quadrant is not important and not urgent. And the bottom right quadrant is not important but very urgent. Most people live in the bottom right quadrant. It's not important but it's highly urgent. These are the things that come across your desk that are someone else's emergency that you have to drop everything and fix. It is not important to you. It might even be a distraction to you, but it's urgent. Then there are many things that fall into the top right quadrant—highly urgent and important. The deadline for that client. The bills getting paid. The sermon for Sunday. An emergency at the hospital that is life or death. These are highly important and highly urgent matters. Pastors tend to live in these two worlds. High urgency, more or less importance. But more often we don't get to move over to the quadrant that really matters—the top left quadrant which is highly important but not urgent. This is the quadrant of visioneering and planning. This is the quadrant of relationship building. This is the quadrant of prayer. And this is the quadrant of disciple making. Chances are good that no one is going to burst into your office tomorrow and say it's vitally urgent that you disciple men right away. It is not urgent. In fact, there are many more things that are urgent. The proposal for the leadership team is urgent. Addressing that blow up on the youth staff is urgent. Stepping into a marriage conflict with one of your leaders is urgent. Disciple making isn't urgent, but it is vitally important. The way you make room for the top left quadrant is you schedule time for it. So I set aside certain times in my week when I am available to meet with men. Most men in our church can meet early in the morning or after dinner. So I have Thursday mornings from 7 a.m. – 9 a.m. blocked off to meet with men. I also have an evening block late on Wednesday nights where I can meet with men. Now, I have to be flexible. These times may have to change. Right now I just finished meeting with two young men who could only meet on Saturday mornings at 7:00a.m., so that's when we met. But I block off times when I am available; that way it happens. If I don't block it off, it won't happen.

**Disciple in stages.** I always found it helpful to start off by asking a man to just give me five weeks. We use a simple tool called, "Lessons on Assurance" produced by The Navigators. It's a very thin piece, simple and direct. But it allows me to start investing in a man's life by showing him the five great assurances we have as followers of Jesus. He is usually not intimidated by the small book and the short amount of time. If he will meet with me for five weeks and he is there faithfully, he is engaged, he comes prepared with his verses memorized, and he's wanting more, then I will continue to invest my time in him using other tools designed to take him deeper. If he is not faithful about showing up and coming prepared, then I won't keep investing in him. I will complete the five weeks and move on to someone else. I look at it this way...I'm giving this man something far more valuable than my money. I'm giving him my life. And if he can't make five weeks with me, then he's not a wise investment of my time. Possibly it is not the right time for him. Maybe he's not ready for that kind of challenge. Either way, I need to move on. Because I have a short piece up front, I can assess the readiness and faithfulness of the man I'm discipling. Find a tool that is only a few weeks long. Use that time to invest in this man and assess his teachable-ness and eagerness. If he wants more, then take him to another level that will require more time and accountability. If he doesn't want more, then cut the line, re-bait, and keep fishing.

**Take them with you.** As I mentioned before, the curriculum or tool is not a substitute for a godly example. Disciple making is about life on life, not getting people through the material. So as you invest in a man, spend time with him, both in ministry and casually. I learned this from David Guinn. When I first met David, he was leading the college ministry for a large church in Waco, Texas. David was a former Olympic wrestler. He was broad and strong, with a full beard and booming voice. David also loved Jesus with all his heart. While running that campus ministry, he led many of the Baylor football players to Christ. God was using him powerfully. Every weekend, hundreds of students at Baylor University would pack into the church to hear him teach the Bible. David was also passionate about making disciples. In fact, it was David who first introduced me to disciple making. He wrote his own material. It was nothing complicated, but it trained students on how to spend time in God's word, to pray, to share their faith, and to love people. I was in Seminary at the time, working with college students, and so I would often ask David to come speak to our group. Every time he would come to speak, I noticed he always had a college athlete with him. Sometimes the student would lead us in a prayer. Sometimes David would have him share his testimony. But David always had a guy with him. When I asked David about it, he said, "Craig, never do ministry alone. Always have a guy with you so you can model for them what ministry looks like." I've never forgotten his words. Ministry and life is more caught than taught. Following David's example, I started discipling students in our college ministry. At the time, Liz and I lived in a small (I mean really small) studio apartment. It was so small you could vacuum the downstairs using one plug! We invited college kids to come over for discipleship on Sunday nights. Looking back, we did it all wrong. We had guys and girls mixed together. We had probably fifteen to twenty crammed into our apartment instead of gathering in small groups. The place was so packed that we had students sitting on the stairs. We practically read through the material with little interaction. We broke all the disciple-making rules. But we invested in their lives. We spent time with them. We had fun together. We went on trips together. We experienced life together. Today, more than half a dozen of those in that group are in full-time ministry, and many more are faithfully making disciples in their churches. As you invest in people, spend time with them. Take them with you as you care for people. Have them over to your house to watch football. Let them see how you interact as a family. Spend time together. Remember, high contact equals high impact.

**Expose them to evangelism opportunities.** Hopefully you know by now that disciple making is not just sitting around a table with a cup of coffee writing in a workbook. Disciple making is imparting your life into another person with the purpose of training them to walk with God, reach their lost friends, and reproduce. As I have already stated, evangelism is the first step in the disciple-making process. Jesus spent roughly half of his earthly ministry in the "come and see" phase, engaging spiritual explorers and confronting them with his claims to be the Christ. When Jesus began discipling his men, he took them on tours throughout the villages in Galilee preaching the gospel. It was as they walked along the way that Jesus invested in their lives, teaching his men and engaging them in conversation. Jesus modeled for his men a love for people far from God. According to Jesus, any real disciple-making strategy must include training men to reach their lost friends with the gospel. So, part of your strategy needs to include helping your men be active, faithful witnesses at home, at the office, on the ball field, and in the neighborhood. Over the years, I've trained men to use the simple "bridge illustration" as a way to present the gospel. Training in evangelism is important, but practice is vital. It is best if you can take the men you are discipling to places where they can practice having spiritual conversations. Any ministry that serves a meal to the homeless or visits men in minimum security prisons or hands out backpacks in local apartments is a great place for men to practice sharing their faith. Also, it's great to encourage your men to invite a lost friend to do something with the two of you. Play golf, go shooting, or take in a ball game together. In this way, you can model how to build relationships and spark spiritual conversations. There are many ways to keep evangelism central in your time with this man. But remember, how you train him is how he will most likely reproduce. If you don't train him in evangelism, he will never train men to actively share their faith. If you show him how to effectively share the gospel, he will do it and train others how to do it for the rest of his life.

## WHAT ARE YOU POURING YOUR LIFE INTO?

In 2011, I was reflecting on the focus of my life. The longer I live, the more I realize how fleeting time is and why Jesus told his disciples, *"We must work the works of him who sent me while it is day; night is coming when no man can work" (John 9.4).* I pulled out a piece of paper and began writing.

» If I pour my life into buildings, they will eventually be torn down.

» If I pour my life into projects, they will come to an end.

» If I pour my life into goals, they will become obsolete.

» If I pour my life into fame, I will soon be forgotten.

» If I pour my life into accomplishments, they will fade.

» If I pour my life into money, it will be spent.

» If I pour my life into possessions, they will belong to someone else.

» If I pour my life into experiences, they will become distant memories.

» If I pour my life into organizations, they will change.

» If I pour my life into products, they will disappear.

» If I pour my life into benevolence, it will be temporary.

» If I pour my life into pleasures, they won't last.

» If I pour my life into wisdom, it will be surpassed.

» If I pour my life into entertainment, it will leave me empty and self-absorbed.

» But if I pour my life into knowing Jesus and training men to help others do the same, then what I do in this life will never fade from the Earth and will echo in eternity.

Every man pours his life into something. What are you pouring your life into? If there was ever a time we needed pastors to make disciples and raise up godly men, the time is now. The church needs you. Men need you. If you will follow the example of Jesus and give yourself to making disciples, your influence will live on in the men who come after you, and your impact will remain until He returns.

I don't know about you, but **I don't want to give my** one and only **life** to **maintaining** an **organization**. However, I would readily **give my life** to **a movement** that **changes people**.

# MOVE FROM INDIVIDUAL TO TEAM

"Give me one hundred men who fear nothing but sin and desire nothing but God, and I care not whether they be clergymen or laymen, they alone will shake the gates of Hell and set up the kingdom of Heaven upon the earth." — John Wesley

Once a leader knows what a disciple looks like and understands Jesus' four-step process for making disciples and begins to actively invest his life in people, then he is ready to raise up a team of disciple makers. Ministry is not something you do in isolation; rather it is something you do in community. Far too often pastors feel alone. In an article titled, "Taking a Break from the Lord's Work," the *New York Times* printed an eye-opening article on the real epidemic of pastor burnout. *"The findings have surfaced with ominous regularity over the last few years, and with little notice: Members of the clergy now suffer from obesity, hypertension and depression at rates higher than most Americans. In the last decade, their use of antidepressants has risen, while their life expectancy has fallen. Many would change jobs if they could."*[13] Over the years, our church has hosted a disciple making conference for pastors. When I talk to many of them, discouragement and loneliness are real issues. I know because I've experienced it firsthand. If you have been a pastor for any length of time, you know what I mean. The pressure to get results, demanding deadlines, unreasonable expectations, divisions in the church, unresolved conflicts, people leaving your church for another one down the street, financial pressures, and struggles at home; all of these can build up walls that imprison and isolate a leader. But ministry was never intended to be done in isolation. Nor was ministry ever intended to be solely the pastor's job. Ministry has always been intended to be done in community, alongside other brothers and sisters in Christ. The role of the pastor is not to do the work of ministry alone, but to equip a team of people to accomplish the work together. The secret to doing ministry together in community and raising up co-laborers is an intentional disciple-making strategy.

---

13    Paul Vittelo, *Taking a Break from the Lord's Work*, New York Times, August 1, 2010.

Jesus taught this principle. In Luke 10.2, Jesus saw the hurting crowd and he told his disciples, *"The harvest is plentiful, but the laborers are few. Therefore pray earnestly to the Lord of the harvest to send out laborers into his harvest."* Jesus didn't say, "The harvest is plentiful but the laborers are few, so I'll just do it myself otherwise it will never get done." But that is what many pastors do. They give in to the notion that no one wants to help and no one cares. But that is simply not true. If you want more laborers in the field, you have to pray for God to send them your way. You have to train them to join you in the work, and then release them to do it. Jesus never envisioned a single laborer in the field trying to get it all in. Can you image that? Picture a massive wheat field, acres and acres of grain ready to be harvested, and only one guy with a sickle in his hand looking at it all. Can you image how discouraging that would be? That's how many pastors feel. Plugging away at the ministry, carrying it completely on his shoulders. Instead, Jesus envisioned many laborers working side by side, bringing in the harvest together. Not only did Jesus teach this principle, he modeled this principle. Jesus worked under the radar engaging spiritual seekers with the truth of his identity. He called men to follow him and drew them into community, exposing them to the ministry (Matthew 4.18-19). He then identified twelve emerging leaders and began to intentionally invest time in them (Mark 3.13-14). He taught them truth, he demonstrated for them the power of God, and he involved them in the ministry at increasingly greater levels. He released them to minister on their own, but with oversight and accountability (Luke 9.1-2). Then he led those leaders to identify and raise up more leaders (Luke 10.1). Soon the twelve became seventy-two, and the seventy-two became one hundred twenty (Acts 1.15). The one hundred twenty, in turn, became five hundred (I Corinthians 15.6). From the very beginning of Jesus' ministry, he was engaging in relationships and bringing them along with him for the purpose of training them and releasing them into the harvest field.

You see the same pattern in the Apostle Paul. From the moment Paul was saved, believers surrounded him. The very people he had sought to imprison and kill in Damascus reached out to him and took him in, even at one point saving Paul's life (Acts 9.19, 25). Barnabas reached out to Paul and invested in his life, ultimately taking Paul to Antioch where they ministered together and raised up a leadership team (Acts 11.25-26; 13.1-3). When the Lord led Paul to take the gospel to the Gentile nations, he didn't go alone. He took men with him. As they traveled, they preached the gospel and established ministry teams (Acts 14.23). He loved these men and poured his life into them. Men like Timothy (I Corinthians 4.17), Titus (2 Corinthians 8.16, 23), Silas (Acts 15.40), Luke (Colossians 4.14; Philemon 1.24), Epaphras (Colossians 4.12), Barnabas (Acts 11.25), Gauis (Romans 16.23), and the elders in Ephesus that he loved so dearly (Acts 20.36-38). When Paul traveled, he was joined by men who were his disciples from various parts of the country (Acts 20.4-

5). When Paul was in prison, he was cared for by the community of believers (Acts 28.11-16). As you read the letters of Paul, he often mentions the people he trained and released into ministry (Romans 16.17-23; 2 Timothy 4.19-22; Colossians 4.7-18). Paul knew that ministry was never to be done in isolation, but in community. He wrote in Ephesians 4.11-12, *"He gave the apostles, the prophets, the evangelists, the shepherds and teachers to equip the saints for the work of ministry, for building up the body of Christ..."* The role of the pastor is to raise up people who will walk with God, reach the world, and invest in a few. Where did these people come from? Initially they came from the people he had personally discipled! That's how Jesus did it. That's how Paul did it. And that's how disciple-making pastors do it today. That is why I love the quote from John Wesley that I placed at the top of this chapter. Wesley was a powerful evangelist. Thousands came to hear him preach, and thousands came to Christ under his itinerate preaching ministry. But the power and genius of Wesley wasn't his preaching, it was his ability to raise up leaders and establish small groups of disciple-making communities all across the nation. Wesley correctly understood that if he had one hundred men who were passionate about Christ and trained to reproduce, there was nothing that could stop them. I still believe that! The only way ministry moves forward is by training up men and then releasing them into the ministry alongside you.

## BUILDING A MINISTRY TEAM

The sun was blazing in the hot Texas sky. It was August, and the high temperatures were well into triple digits. From a distance, you could see the heat waves rising from the cracked Texas soil. By the late afternoon, trucks and cars came streaming onto a remote ranch. Once you passed the first gate and crossed several cattle guards, you followed a winding trail leading to a clear pasture where men began to assemble their tents. As the sun was setting, close to one hundred men were eating barbeque and playing capture the flag with paint guns. Soon the place was black with night. The stars reflected their brilliant constellations in the sky, and the men were sitting encircling a central lantern. This was not just an ordinary gathering. These were not just ordinary men. These were men who had made the choice to invest their lives in other men. Each were men who were proven reproducers, proven multipliers. I stood in the circle and began telling these men the secret to the power of the Roman Army. "The Centuria was the basic tactical unit of the Roman army during the life of Christ. It was comprised of eighty warriors. Within the Centuria, the eighty fighting men were broken down into ten groups of eight called "contubernia." These eight warriors slept in tents together, worked together, trained together, ate together, and fought back-to-back together. They were committed to advancing the kingdom of Rome, doing the hard work in the trenches, and fighting hand-to-hand combat. They were the heroes. They were the "tip of the spear." Each man's eyes were glued to mine. Their hearts were receiving every word. "This is why tonight I am calling you Centuria. You are the personally trained and battled-tested warriors of our church! You know how to make disciples. You are the special forces. You are the tip of the spear. You are the front line warriors of the movement that God is producing in and through us. David had his mighty men. Joshua had his warriors. Jesus had his trained disciples. I have you! And our mission is simple: we are called by our Commander and King, Jesus Christ, to reproduce ourselves in the lives of men by making disciples who make disciples. We are called to walk with God, to reach the world, and to invest in a few." You could almost feel the adrenaline surging through the men's veins. Before the night was over, each man would stand beside a campfire and receive a challenge coin. On the coin was the commitment to walk, reach, and invest. "Will you commit to make disciples until Jesus comes?" I would ask. They would each reply, "Yes I will!"

There is something compelling and life-giving about a clear call and comrades. Most men go through life accomplishing tasks but never accomplishing much. We don't live in a day where there are battles to be waged. There is very little in this life that calls us to something greater than ourselves. That is what Jesus did with his men. He called them away from small thinking and self-absorbed living to a greater cause. He called them to give their lives to something that really mattered, to a movement that would change the world. When you give yourself to make disciples, you help them reproduce. Eventually you will gather a group of like-minded men who, as Wesley said, can "shake the gates of hell." How do you build a team of men like that? How do you develop men who will work shoulder-to-shoulder with you in the trenches of disciple making?

Here are some practical things to keep in mind.

**Identify your disciple makers.** A ministry team needs to be comprised of people who are faithfully making disciples using your preferred tools. Not everyone whom you disciple will reproduce in others. I wish that wasn't the case, but it is reality. In Matthew 13, Jesus told us this would be the case. In the story of the sower, the seed of God's Word responds differently in different soils. In some soils the seed doesn't produce any fruit at all. In other soils the fruit is very productive! The moral of the story is simply this: not everyone will reproduce what you plant in his or her life. Some will receive what you say but it will never take root in their lives. Some will hear God's Word planted in them but be choked out by the distractions and demands of life. And some will take God's Word that you invest in their lives and share it with others, producing a great harvest of spiritual multiplication. Not everyone you train will reproduce. Jesus said so. I've been making disciples for twenty years. It has been my experience that one out of every four men I train will actually continue to reproduce over the long haul. That's not discouraging to me, it's just reality. So, if that's true, I need to be constantly looking for the men who are passionate about walking with God, reaching the lost, and investing in a few, and I need to stay close to them. If you are privileged to have a paid staff working alongside you, then begin with them. Invest in them, train them to reproduce, and set them free to do it with encouragement and accountability. I expect every staff member on our team to be a disciple maker. There are many in our church who are not on paid staff, but are proven disciple makers. These are the men who were in the circle on that warm Texas night. These men are my proven reproducers. Some of these men have gone on to lead groups and serve on leadership teams. Others God led to quit their jobs and come on staff at the church. Still others changed their work schedules so they could spend more time investing in men. This is my disciple-making ministry team. Now you may be thinking, "I wish I had a group of dedicated men like that." You can! But you have to build them. You build them by discipling them yourself and helping them to reproduce. Over time, your proven reproducers will begin to grow. Then that group becomes your team that will move your ministry forward. I encourage you to identify who these people are in your church and draw close to them. These are the men Wesley was talking about. Spend time with them. Keep them encouraged. Focus them on outreach strategies in your church. Constantly funnel new believers to them so they are always discipling. Inspire them with stories of success, reminding them of the eternal impact they are making.

**Clarify your purpose.** As you are building your team, keep the mission of the church central. The mission of every church is to make disciples who make disciples. However you word it, that should be the essence of your mission statement. Jesus made the mission crystal clear to his disciples. In Matthew 28.18, Jesus said, *"Go make disciples of all nations."* It was clear. It was compelling. They understood it. That is the mission of Jesus and that is the mission of every church. The mission statement at our church is simply, "Igniting movements that transform people into thriving followers of Jesus Christ." Let me break that down for you. First, our mission is to ignite movements. We aren't about maintaining programs. We aren't about focusing on ourselves. We are movement catalysts. We believe that Jesus ignited a powerful movement two thousand years ago and we are joining him in fueling that movement all around the world. People don't get excited about maintaining an organization, but people get excited about being part of a movement. As Steve Addison says, *"Movements change people and people change the world."*[14] What kind of movement are we engaged in? We are part of a movement that "transforms people into thriving followers of Jesus Christ." This movement is about life transformation. It takes us the way we are and transforms us by the power of the gospel into thriving (vibrant, growing, reproducing) followers of Jesus. I don't know about you, but I don't want to give my one and only life to maintaining an organization. However,

---

14    *Movements That Change the World*, Steve Addison, page 29.

I would readily give my life to a movement that changes people. Keeping the mission clear and keeping the mission central is the most important part of the leader's responsibility. Why is this important? Because if the mission isn't central, your church will drift from its mission or competing missions will arise and bring confusion. Every church is susceptible to this. Personalities with personal agendas can hijack the mission. Programs that have a long-standing tradition can undermine the mission. Trends and fads can circumvent the mission. But when the mission is lost, so is the church. In Oklahoma City, there was a night club just a few miles from the church where I served. What's unique about this night club is that it used to be a church. Years ago that church was planted by a few passionate followers of Jesus who wanted to be a light for Christ in that neighborhood. Believers gathered and prayed. They reached out to their community and shared the gospel. Leaders were raised up and the church began to grow. Eventually the pastor called the small church to sacrifice and give financially to build a building for the glory of God. The people gave, the building was constructed, and the people celebrated. Now even more people were coming to the church. Organizations were formed. Structures were put in place. Traditions were made. Programs were established. But then something happened. My guess is that it happened so quietly, so silently, that no one even noticed. At some point, the people stopped reaching out to their community. They lost sight of their initial mission. The focus shifted to retaining members and upholding traditions rather than preaching the gospel and making disciples. The church began to decline. Some people left the church. Others in the congregation simply grew old and died off. Then one day the church closed its doors. Only the structure remained. Once, it was a beacon of hope to its community, and now it was a dilapidated, empty shell. Then an investor came along and saw an opportunity. He took the church building and turned it into a night club. He called it Purgatory. It became one of the darkest and most dangerous night clubs in the city. The rumor was that police would be called to that club on a regular basis and they entered at their own risk. That club became a hotspot for violence and drug use. What once was a place of light and hope became a place of darkness and destruction. I keep a picture of that night club framed in my office. To me, it's a stark reminder of what happens when a church loses sight of its mission to make disciples. Keep the mission clear and central.

**Cast clear and compelling vision.** Now is the time to cast vision. Pastor, if you are itching to preach on disciple making, now is the time. Jesus was a master at casting vision. When his disciples were with him in Samaria, Jesus said, *"Look I tell you, lift up your eyes and see that the fields are white for harvest"* (John 4.35). On another occasion, Jesus said, *"Truly, truly I say to you, unless a grain of wheat falls into the earth and dies, it remains alone; but if it dies, it bears much fruit"* (John 12.24). On the night before his death, Jesus took a cluster of grapes in his hands and told them, *"I am the vine; you are the branches. Whoever abides in me and I in him, he it is that bears much fruit, for apart from me you can do nothing"* (John 15.5). In all these images, Jesus was casting vision of multiplication. "Look up," Jesus said. "When people come to me it is like a huge harvest that's ready to be taken in. Look, spiritual multiplication happens when you die to yourself, like this seed of wheat. Only then can God use you to reproduce. Look, you are like this cluster of grapes. Attached to me you can and will bear fruit and make disciples." Jesus was the master communicator. In the same way, it is the leader's responsibility to cast a clear and compelling vision for disciple making. If you cast vision before you actually make disciples, then your vision will be nothing more than an idea or wishful thinking. But if you wait until you have actually made a few disciples and have seen them reproduce, then you will have real stories to share of how God is using you and others to reach people for Christ and walk with them to maturity. The vision becomes tangible. The vision has skin on it. Sometimes it is helpful to craft a vision statement. Unlike the mission statement, which is short and succinct, the vision statement is oftentimes a more robust statement describing what the mission will look like when it is implemented in your local church context. What will people see when the mission becomes a reality? A compelling vision is the most lethal weapon a leader has in his arsenal. Vision creates motivation. Vision creates momentum. Vision inspires. Vision excites. Without a compelling vision, the people are set adrift to follow their own whims and interests, and the church suffers. There are several ways to communicate vision. You can cast vision one-on-one. This is something I try to do regularly when I meet with leaders over lunch or coffee. Even though I know they are on the team, I need to be constantly casting the vision of where we are going and what we are doing, giving them examples of successes along the way. Vision casting needs to happen also at the church staff level. I meet with our entire staff team once a week for worship and prayer. Part of that gathering is sharing successes in ministry and celebrating each department's success. It's great fun and there is usually a lot of laughter and ribbing going on. But I make sure on a regular basis to remind them of the vision. We are here for one purpose only and that is to join Jesus in his movement to make disciples. You can cast vision to your disciple makers. That group which is committed to making disciples needs a fresh dose of vision and encouragement to keep the fires burning. I try to gather that group together several times a year for just that purpose. You can cast vision to all your volunteers in the church. Everyone who is serving at any capacity, whether that's in the baby nursery or as a parking attendant or part of the worship team. Everyone needs to gather together and be inspired with a fresh dose of vision and encouragement. Finally, you can cast vision to your congregation through preaching. You may choose certain times during the year to craft a special vision-casting message that imparts what making disciples looks like in the church and features stories of how that is happening in your church. Suddenly, the vision isn't theoretical, it's extremely practical and exciting. Everyone is inspired when a Christ-exalting, Spirit-energizing, church-empowering vision is cast. Vision gives purpose to our labor and meaning to our sacrifice.

**Communicate a simple disciple-making process.** As you clarify your mission and cast a compelling vision, it's important to communicate in a simple way your strategic plan for making disciples. Your strategic plan should mirror the four-step process of Jesus in simple terms so people can easily identify where they are and what their next steps should be. The trick here is simplicity. I remember early on in ministry when I was learning the life of Christ, I put together a beautiful, multi-colored brochure articulating our four-step disciple-making strategy. I was so proud of it. It was thoughtful, intentional, accurate, and insightful. As I remember, it folded out like a road map! However, it was way too complicated! People looked at it and their eyes rolled back in their heads. I look back on that now and laugh. I was right in my content, but got it completely wrong in my presentation. Don't make my mistake. Keep things simple. Our strategic plan is summarized in four words: Explore, Connect, Grow, and Go. Everything we do falls into one of those categories. The Explore phase helps people far from God explore the claims of Christ and find answers to their spiritual questions. The Connect Phase helps believers connect with Christ, the church, a community, and a cause. The Grow Phase helps people grow up in their faith and trains them to be and build disciples of Christ. The Go Phase helps people make disciples who make disciples where they live, learn, work, and play. I can draw that out on a napkin. It's very simple. Every great disciple-making church or ministry is able to clearly lay out their strategic plan for making disciples and communicate it to their church. Not everyone in the seats will get it. That's okay. They just need to know where they are and what their next step should be. But your staff, leaders, and disciple makers need to understand it completely. Clarify and simplify your strategic plan. Stay focused on it. Hardwire this plan into everything you do. And as you teach the life of Christ, show that this was Jesus' plan all along.

One way to clarify your mission, vision, and strategic plan for making disciples is to develop a "Leadership Dashboard." This is a one- or two-page summary of your mission, vision, and strategic process. Whether you have a large, full-time paid staff or you are working with volunteers, the responsibility of the leader is to keep the mission, vision, and process of disciple making front and center. Often a simple summary is very helpful. I've sat on the board of multi-million dollar organizations, and I've discovered that the larger the organization and the more complicated the structure, the simpler the communication. It's the old KISS method: "keep it simple stupid." Create what works for you. Keep it clear and concise. Make sure it's simple. Then communicate it all the time.

**Celebrate when people take the next step in the process.** People do what gets celebrated. We are just hardwired that way. What gets affirmed gets done. Therefore, make celebration a big part of the culture of your church. Celebrate significant milestones in a person's spiritual journey. For example, when a person leads a friend to Christ, find a way to celebrate that. When a person crosses the line of faith and is baptized, make sure the baptism is a big celebration of what God has done. When a person joins the church, that's cause for celebration. When someone joins a group, it's time to celebrate. When a person completes the phase of discipleship training, that's a big reason to celebrate. When a person reproduces into the life of another person, celebrate! Find ways to celebrate milestones at every step along the spiritual pathway. The reason I say this is because I don't think we celebrate enough. Many churches are all about the "push" of guilt and intimidation. People do things because they feel pushed. But a healthy church is about the "pull" of celebration. People want to step up to the next level, because when they do they are celebrated and cheered along the way. Think about it. Would you rather feel guilty or celebrated? Would you want to do something because if you don't there will be reprisals, or would you rather do something because when you do the room will explode with applause? Jesus talked about the power of celebration. He said that whenever one sinner repents, all of heaven bursts into celebration. *"Just so, I tell you, there will be more joy* in *heaven over one sinner who repents than over ninety-nine righteous persons who need no repentance."* (Luke 15.7). Jesus said that at the end of time, when he comes again and gathers up his own to be with him forever that there will be a huge banquet celebration (Luke 14.16-17; Revelation 19.6-10). When Jesus saw his twelve multiply into seventy-two, Jesus was filled with joy (Luke 10.21). Jesus celebrated this huge accomplishment and how God was working in and through them. Even when Jesus was moving toward the cross and he knew his death was imminent, he was not pushed to the cross out of sheer obedience and obligation, but he was pulled toward the cross because of the joy he would experience on the other side in heaven. Hebrews 12.2 says, *"who for the joy that was set before him endured the cross, despising the shame, and is seated at the right hand of the throne of God."* Jesus knew that when he stepped out of this world and into heaven as the conquering king and resurrected Lord, all of heaven would celebrate with him! Nowhere do you see Jesus using guilt and intimidation to get people to follow him. People always had a way out if they wanted it, but Jesus celebrated every step forward. I think celebration and affirmation are the two most powerful tools in a disciple-maker's tool belt. In a day when people are pushed and beaten down, what they need and long for is someone to celebrate them! So find creative ways to infuse celebration into every layer of the church.

**Place disciple makers in positions of leadership.** Jesus didn't turn the reins of the movement over to men who were just great leaders. He turned it over to men he had personally trained and who had been with him from the beginning (Acts 10.39-40; Matthew 10.1-4; Mark 6.40). Those who were chosen as apostles in the early church were men who had known Jesus and walked with Jesus. This was the purpose for which they were trained. Jesus invested his life in these men so that they would lead the movement he started. The same is true in the church. Those who lead the movement should be people who have been trained and proven themselves faithful in making disciples. Why would you want someone leading your organization who doesn't believe or embody its stated purpose? As more people are discipled through your ministry and begin to exhibit the life of a disciple, then elevate those with leadership gifts to positions of leadership so they can help you carry on the work. It has been my experience that most church conflicts on staff and on elder boards are tied to a difference in ministry philosophy. Opinions cross, tempers flare, and relationships are broken because they fundamentally don't agree on what the church should be doing or where it should be going. However, when you disciple men and women and then elevate them to areas of influence and leadership because they have proven themselves faithful, the probability of conflict over ministry philosophy is diminished and the church as a whole walks together in unity. Don't get me wrong, I'm not saying there will be no conflict. Even among good-hearted, disciple-making people, tempers can rise. Paul's conflict with Barnabas created a rift that lasted years (Acts 15.39). The conflict over the inclusion of Gentiles into the church necessitated the first church council (Acts 15.1-31). But even in these times of conflict, believers were able to come to a resolution because fundamentally they agreed on the mission, vision, and strategy of Jesus. I strongly believe that when the pastor, staff, and leaders are all on the same page regarding the mission, vision, and strategy of the church, there is more peace and less conflict.

**Pray together as a team.** Jesus led his team to constantly seek the Father in prayer. Immediately after appointing his leadership team, Jesus sat down and gave them a sermon. It many ways, it was their ordination sermon into the ministry. Part of that sermon was on how to pray (Matthew 6.5-13). He launched them into the ministry in prayer. Sporadically, throughout their time together, when the pace would get fast and the hours would get long, Jesus would pull them back to rest and pray (Matthew 14.22-23; Luke 5.16, 9.10, 18; Mark 3.7, 6.31-34; 45-46 John 6.14-15). When the ministry was short on workers and resources, Jesus told them to pray (Matthew 9.35-38). When they encountered resistance from the enemy, he told them to pray (Matthew 17.14-21; Mark 9.14-29). When big decisions had to be made, Jesus modeled prayer (Mark 3.13-19). When the sun went down he prayed (Mark 1.32). When he was tempted he prayed (Luke 4.1-13). When he was grieving he prayed (John 11.40-44). When people pressed close to him for ministry, he prayed (Mark 10.16). Toward the end of his ministry, as Jesus was coming closer to the cross, he reminded them how they should pray (Luke 11.1). He told them to be persistent in prayer (Luke 10.1-10). During his last moments with his men, Jesus prayed over them (John 17.1-26), and in the Garden of Gethsemane Jesus asked them to pray with him (Luke 22.39-46). Jesus saturated his ministry and his men with prayer. I don't think the importance of prayer in your church can be overstated. Likewise, I don't think that anything you do will be eternally impactful and effective apart from fervent and frequent prayer. I encourage you to lead your church to seek the Lord in prayer. In prayer we are expressing our dependence on God. In prayer we are drawing close to hear his voice and receive his instruction. In prayer we are seeking his power to embolden us and empower us. All of that happens when God's people pray. At our church we have really put effort into leading our people to pray. As a church staff we meet every week and worship together, study God's Word together, and pray. We've committed to spending as much time in prayer and the word as we do in staff meeting. We set aside special weekends throughout the year to focus our entire church on prayer. We host Encounter Services, designed to engage the people in worship based prayer. In these services the entire time is designed to lead people to worship God and seek him in prayer. It is a highly interactive and participative experience. We sponsor prayer walks in our community and pray over neighborhoods and businesses. I guess the more I seek to make disciples that will change the world, the more I realize that I can't do it apart from God's Spirit moving and changing hearts. Disciple making leads to desperate praying.

God never called you to do this ministry alone. He called you to do it in community. As you invest your life in people and raise up spiritual multipliers, you will find that God will give you the team you need to accomplish the vision he has put in your heart.

I don't think that anything you do will be **eternally impactful** and effective apart from **fervent** and **frequent prayer**.

You **can't improve** what you **can't measure**. How can you make **informed decisions** about the **effectiveness** of any ministry **if you don't measure it?**

# MOVE FROM TRADITION TO EVALUATION

Once you have established your definition of a disciple, hard-wired your process, begun to live it out personally, and raised up a disciple-making team, you will be ready to begin to evaluate the programs in your church. Let's be honest. Most programs begin with good intentions, but over time these programs can become dated and ineffective, slowly turning into sacred cows or entrenched traditions. These programs usually garner tremendous support. They are often vigorously championed, and are highly charged with emotion. Every church has programs like this. It is easy to just keep doing them because we have always done them. But a disciple-making church is constantly evaluating the effectiveness of every program, event or initiative and asking the hard questions: "What part of the strategy is this accomplishing?" "Is this really working?" "Is there a better way to be more effective?"

## FATAL ATTRACTION

Traditions are not bad. In fact they can be incredibly powerful. We have certain traditions in our house that we have kept for years. Every Christmas Eve, our family gathers for a special lunch. We always eat the same things: Cornish hens, stuffing, veggies, sparkling cider, and some great dessert. It's our tradition. At that time, the girls always get their first Christmas gifts, which are traditionally always pajamas. We also read passages written on cards about the birth of Jesus and light the candles on an Advent wreath. Then we clean up and head out for a long evening of Christmas Eve services. It's our tradition. We have done it for over twenty years, and we love it. Traditions are powerful because they have a way of reinforcing values and passing down truths from one generation to the next. That is why God proscribed that the Jewish people celebrate certain feasts and festivals throughout the year. They were strongly held traditions intended to pass on spiritual truths to the next generation. Of course, over time, the Jewish people developed all kinds of traditions that were added to the biblical mandates. I can't help but think about Tevye's opening monologue in the musical, "Fiddler on the Roof." *"We have traditions for everything. How to sleep, how to eat, how to work, how to wear clothes. For instance we always keep our heads covered and always wear a little prayer shawl. This shows our constant devotion to God. You may ask, 'How did this traditions get started?' And I'll tell you...I don't know. But it's a tradition."* Every time I hear that monologue I smile because it's so true, especially in churches. We have a knack for doing one thing, and if it's successful then we keep doing it, regardless of the long-term effectiveness, until we drive it into the ground. It's a tradition. These traditions may involve certain musical performances, how people dress, the order of a service, the locations of certain groups, or the use of certain facilities. If we are not careful, our traditions can get in the way of accomplishing the church's mission. A good friend told me recently about how one church was reaching many young families. So many were coming that there was no more room for these families to meet in groups on campus. The pastor noticed a formal parlor in the church sitting unused and proposed that the room be renovated for this new, growing segment of the church. Plans were drawn, bids were let, and contractors were appointed. But at the last minute, a large donor who initially gave money for the parlor to be built years ago privately protested to the lead pastor. Immediately, the job was scrapped and the parlor stayed intact and vacant. Every church has traditions. There is nothing wrong with that. But when those traditions become obstacles to making disciples, then we have a problem. While that is obvious to most leaders, knowing how to navigate the turbulent waters of change can be extremely difficult and hazardous. I knew one pastor in Oklahoma City who stepped into a dying church. Before long, he was reaching out into the community and bringing new people into the aged congregation. For the first time in years, baptisms were up and people were joining. That's all good, right? Wrong. The pastor was quickly fired because the parishioners didn't want "those people" coming into their church. That, my friend, is the death rattle of any congregation. The moment traditions matter more than the mission, the church is on the way down. Most cases are not so obvious. Maybe a men's event needs to be stopped so that another initiative can begin. Maybe a Christmas program is waning in impact and needs to be refreshed or replaced. Maybe the church needs to rework its worship style, group strategy, or leadership development plan. How do you go about changing the culture of a church to become more aligned with disciple making? That's what I'm going to share with you in this chapter. You see, some things will have to go in order for new things to come. You simply can't continue to add new plans, new initiatives, and new strategies and maintain the old ones at the same time. Why? Because you don't have unlimited resources. You don't have unlimited time, unlimited money, unlimited volunteers, unlimited capital, unlimited space, and unlimited talent. So if you are going to make disciples, you are going to have to leverage the resources you do have in the most effective way possible. To accomplish this means things in your church will eventually have to change.

# THE DANGER OF MISALIGNMENT

Let's just say it out loud. We are addicted to programs. We are tied to our traditions. Just as an addict reacts emotionally when weaned off of his drug, people react negatively when their favorite program is changed or canceled. This reality has kept even the bravest leaders from making necessary changes lest they find themselves looking for other employment! So, why risk it? Why make changes? The answer is the danger of misalignment. Ask your mechanic what happens when your tires are misaligned. Ultimately, the excess rub and drag of one tire misaligned will lead to a blowout. I remember sitting in a leadership training seminar. They showed us a picture of a championship rowing team. Each team member was in his place, rowing in perfect precision. Each one was doing exactly his part. They were completely aligned to accomplish their goal. Now imagine the same team, but this time one member is out of sync. His oar is colliding with the others or dragging in the water too long. Maybe he doesn't like facing in the same direction as everyone else and wants to change his seat. What is he doing? His misalignment is hurting the team and ultimately the cause. When you have programming that is good, but is not aligned to your disciple-making philosophy of ministry, it hurts the team and the cause. Misalignment is dangerous. For example, misaligned programs distract. They distract people from being involved in the mission-critical initiatives. Misaligned programs dilute resources. Finances, facilities, and leadership given to these programs take away from more important and effective plans. Misaligned programs clutter the schedule and compete for promotional time. Misaligned programs are not strategic. They move by their own inertia, not because they make a significant contribution to the direction of the church. Misaligned programs are often "off limits" to any critical assessment. Their results and effectiveness are seldom evaluated.

What can be done about the misalignment in your church? Well, I don't recommend that you unilaterally decide what needs to change and announce it from the platform on Sunday. Abrupt changes only engender defensiveness and conflict. Don't say, "I've decided we are going to be a disciple-making church and so we are going to scrap all that we have been doing and go in a new direction." That might be your last sermon. Even Jesus drew a hostile reaction in Nazareth when he proposed a change in their thinking. The better way is to lead your church to embrace and celebrate a culture of ongoing evaluation. Let me explain.

## KEY STEPS TO PLANNING AND EVALUATING MINISTRY

A healthy church is constantly evaluating its programming to ensure that it is producing fully mature and reproducing disciples. You are clear on your final product: a 3D disciple. You are clear on the four-step process for making disciples: Explore, Connect, Grow, and Go. You have effectively discipled men and women who are faithfully reproducing, moving many of them into leadership positions. Now you are ready to move into the evaluation stage. Let me give you some fundamental thoughts to consider.

## PLAN WITH THE PROCESS IN MIND

As a disciple-making pastor, your goal is to produce disciples by moving people through the four phases of Jesus' disciple-making process. This is how Jesus made disciples. In a perfect world, you want effective programs working at every phase in your church. For example, in the Explore Phase, you would want effective strategies in place to help you engage those far from God with the claims of Christ and help them find answers to their spiritual questions. In the Connect Phase, you want key initiatives in place that help people cross the line of faith, join the church, get baptized, find a group, and get involved in service. In the Grow Phase, you would want actionable plans designed to help train believers to walk with God, reach their world, and invest in a few. In the Go Phase you want programs that help people multiply themselves spiritually in the lives of others, as well as promote group and church multiplication. A healthy church will have effective programs at every phase in the process. Underline and star that last sentence. I've discovered that most churches don't have a clear definition of what they are making, don't have a clear process, and therefore don't have balance at every stage. Dr. Dann Spader surveyed 100 churches and asked them to describe their programming. He then dropped their programs into the appropriate phases. According to his research, he found that 88% of those surveyed had ALL of their programming at the Connect Phase. All of their programming was to connect and build up believers. There was no intentional programming to reach the lost. No intentional programming to train people to reproduce. No intentional programming to multiply the ministry. He called this the 88 percent problem. When I came to the church in Colleyville, we evaluated our programming and found the same thing. Most churches offer programs for Christians to help them pray, read their bibles, and connect with other Christians, but they are not offering much in the other three phases. I suggest that in the beginning, you pull out a piece of paper and draw four vertical columns down the page. Place the headings Explore, Connect, Grow, and Go on each column. Then categorize all the programs you are currently doing under the appropriate heading. Remember that each program can only have one primary purpose. In other words, you can't say, for example, worship has the purpose of helping explorers, building believers, and training people. You can only pick one primary purpose. Once you have listed and categorized your programming, then evaluate it. Which phase has the most programming? Which phase has the least? Which areas need to be thinned out, and which areas need additional attention? Remember, offering effective programming at each phase is critical to moving people through the disciple-making process.

# CHOOSE METRICS AT EACH PHASE

Once you have programming at each phase, then you want to decide how you will measure success (see Appendix). Let's say your student ministry has a weekly event on Wednesday night categorized as an Explore event. Placing this event here means that the event's primary purpose is to help spiritual explorers hear the claims of Christ and find answers to their spiritual questions. Now the question becomes, "Is this event actually being effective?" To answer this question you will have to determine which metrics you will use to measure success at this phase. What is a metric? A metric is a measurement by which you can determine the success of a given event, activity, or program. Metrics allow you to assess the effectiveness of your ministry, track your progress, and make informed decisions. In the Explore Phase, metrics may include: How many unchurched people attended the event? How many believers actually shared the gospel at the event? How many spiritual conversations were there? How many people responded to the gospel? These metrics will provide you with a clear, unbiased assessment of your outreach ministry. Then, based on this information, what adjustments if any need to be made to make this program more effective? Metrics are extremely helpful because they are the gauges that tell you if the strategies and programs you are using are actually working. I strongly believe that metrics should be established for every program in your church. Listen, you can't improve what you can't measure. How can you make informed decisions about the effectiveness of any ministry if you don't measure it?

Many pastors and leaders have shied away from using metrics. They argue that this approach is too secular. I've heard them say, "The church is not a business." However, I find it odd that I sit on the board of a multi-million dollar company that services people's temporary needs and rigorously measures every step in its process, but the church, which has been entrusted with the gospel that affects people's eternity, refuses to do so. We are in business—our Father's business—and we need to lead like all eternity is counting on it. I think, in reality, pastors often don't want to measure programming because they are afraid of what it will reveal. Once metrics are in place, then the truth of the ministry's real effectiveness will be known. It's much easier to stay busy and be thought of as successful, than to measure the results and know the truth. Every year we look at metrics for success in our ministries, and every year certain staff members grumble a bit because of the results. Every year I remind our team, "Facts are our friends." If a ministry is trending up, we can celebrate and ask how we can keep it going. If a ministry is trending down, then we pray and ask how we can improve or what changes need to be made. The results are not a reflection on the leader's personal worth or value, they simply show the leader what areas need special attention. Remember, facts are your friends. Embrace brutal honesty in your ministry. Ask God to give you creative insight as you gather data, analyze trends, and lead your church toward greater effectiveness.

## SET CLEAR GOALS

Once you have determined your programming at each phase in the disciple-making process and you have assessed each ministry's effectiveness, it's time to make adjustments and set goals. Once again, there are many pastors who refuse to set any kind of goal at all. "How can you put a goal on what God wants to do?" they will say. They may even get biblical and say something like, "Neither Jesus nor Paul ever set goals!" But I disagree. I think Jesus and Paul both set clear, huge, audacious goals. A careful study of Jesus' ministry reveals that Jesus had some clear objectives he felt compelled to accomplish. In Mark chapter one, Jesus is ministering to large crowds that gathered to experience his healing touch. Early the next morning, while it was still dark, Jesus got up and went to a quiet place to pray. By daybreak the disciples were looking for him. They said, "Jesus, everyone is looking for you!" There was already a line of people waiting to be healed by Jesus. But Jesus said to them, *"Let us go on to the next towns, that I may preach there also, for that is why I came out"* (Mark 1.38). Jesus had been directed by his Father to preach the gospel in all the Jewish villages in Galilee. He had a clear objective and because it was clear, he was able to make hard decisions. I'm sure it was difficult to explain walking away from hurting people. Healing was certainly a good thing to do. But sometimes the "good" can be the enemy of the "best." Through prayer, Jesus was able to discern his priorities and set a clear goal that would further his mission. The Apostle Paul did the same thing. In his letter to the church at Rome, Paul revealed that he had often attempted to come to Rome to preach the gospel, but had been hindered in doing so. However, he was planning to arrive soon and then from there he had his sights set on traveling to Spain (Romans 15.22-24). It was clear that both Jesus and Paul had Spirit-directed goals born out of times of prayer as they sought the Father for direction. I believe that every church leader should plan their ministry, evaluate their ministry, and then pray for God to give them fresh Spirit-directed goals for their ministry. In our church, we set goals after periods of prayer. These goals should fit a certain criteria. First, they need to be SMART goals. The acronym S.M.A.R.T. has been used in business circles for years. Goals should be specific, measurable, attainable, realistic, and time-bound. In other words, don't make the goal so general that you wouldn't know if you hit it or not. The goals of Jesus and Paul were clear. They were committed to going to a certain place, by a certain time, to accomplish a certain thing. I have found that leaders will often hide behind generalized goals so that they will not be exposed for having missed that goal. A goal for a Wednesday night youth outreach event should not be to "have a good time" or even to "glorify God." How can you assess whether these things even happened? A better goal would be to have fifty percent of the crowd there be seekers and clearly share the gospel with ten people. That goal is clear and specific. Second, make sure your goals are moving the ministry forward and not just articulating an action item. For example, "setting up the band" is not a goal for your Wednesday night event. That is simply an action item that needs to be done. The goal would be to clearly articulate the gospel to a certain number of people that night. The first is a thing to do, the latter is the goal that drives the ministry forward. Third, your goals should stretch your faith. Many leaders make their goals small so they are sure to accomplish them, but small goals never stretch your faith, and they never change the world. Ask God to give you a large faith goal. Ask God to give you courage to stretch for something that you have never done before. Dream big. Exercise your faith. Ask God for sea-splitting, wall-crumbling, giant-dropping, lion-stopping, audacious faith to see Him do what only He can do. If you don't reach your goal, my guess is you will still have made tremendous progress. Fourth, your goals should come with accountability. Someone must be responsible for each of the goals. Ownership is important. This is not the time for blame-shifting, excuse-making, or deferred responsibility. We are about Kingdom business. King Jesus has entrusted to us his gospel with the clear, unrelenting command to make disciples of all nations. Let's give our best to accomplish this in our lifetime!

## CARVE OUT TIME FOR EVALUATION

Planning and goal setting require time and concentrated effort. You may be thinking, "How can I find time to do this while I'm already stretched for time as it is?" I recommend that you plan your ministry and set your goals once a year, and then you evaluate your progress three times a year. At our church, we carve out about six weeks in the early summer to gather in teams and assess the effectiveness of our ministry. Usually during this time, I'm asking God to reveal to me fresh vision and new initiatives. We look at our programming, we track our progress, we pray, and we make decisions regarding changes for the next ministry year. We write down what our programs will be for the next year, how we will measure success, and our Spirit-directed goals. Early on, we would allot a week to work on these things. We soon realized that we needed more time for prayer, reflection, and collaboration, so we expanded that to about six weeks. I recommend that you not rush the process. Things take time. You want to be sure that when you are done, everyone on your leadership team has had input and ownership in the process. This is not the time for you as the leader to mandate every detail. Guide the process with good questions and give each team member permission to be part of the assessment and planning. After all, if they are not on board from the beginning, they will not be willing do what it takes to make the plans successful. We start in the summer and then all of these plans go into effect the first week of September. From that point forward, we are focused on executing the plans. However, if you don't stop to assess how you are doing, those plans will quickly begin to collect dust on the shelf, ignored by the heavy demands and pace of ministry. Accordingly, you will need to carve out times throughout the year to go back and evaluate, create, and/or renovate your plans in real time. Our church tends to operate on trimesters, matching the school system in our community. We have a strong Fall, beginning in September, but things die down after Christmas. Then we have a strong surge again in January, with things starting to wind down by late Spring. Then we move into the summer months; this is a different animal altogether with lots of our people traveling. In light of that, we have organized our church programming into trimesters: September-December, January-April, May-August. We plan our programming by trimesters, and we set our goals by trimester, and we stop to evaluate at the beginning of every trimester. So, we will stop in January and spend about week in various meetings looking at our goals, assessing what worked, tracking our progress, identifying problems and making adjustments for the next trimester. We will do this again in May and in July. Evaluating three times a year keeps everyone on track and pulling in the same direction. A common business acronym for this process is P.D.C.A., which stands for plan, do, check, act. Usually these words are written in a circle on a whiteboard with arrows between each word, one leading into the next. First you plan the ministry, then you do it. Along the way, you determine times to check your progress and then act accordingly, adjusting when necessary. It is absolutely critical as the leader that you are engaging your team in this process. Most people I know want to do a good job. They want to be successful. They want to fulfill their ministry. Sometimes evaluations can be intimidating. However, I've discovered that if your team is engaged in every part of this process—drafting plans, establishing metrics, setting goals, and assessing progress, then they feel like a valued member of the team with skin in the game, rather than an employee being told what to do. Remember – engage, don't impose.

## NO SUDDEN MOVES

As you go through this process of planning and evaluating, ultimately you will discover that some programs are not aligned with your mission to make disciples. They are "good" things to do, but they are not the "best" things to do. This is where you will come face to face with the stayed traditions and sacred cows. Oftentimes this can feel like the standoff at the OK Corral—you staring down a leader who is committed to an event or program that needs to go. Before you allow things to get contentious, remember that it is your job to love and shepherd your people. People in churches are like people on planes, they don't like sudden moves. Now, some changes are not big at all, and they can be made rather quickly with only a few conversations. But some changes are big and require lots of conversation and consensus before you can move forward. If you are facing a change like that, then remember the phrase I used earlier, "Facts are your friends." Show how you have been tracking the progress of the given program. Demonstrate the amount of time, man hours, and resources that go into the program and how ineffective it is in accomplishing the goal. Once you have made the case that the current plan isn't working, then begin to offer solutions and cast vision. "What if we could do something that would be really effective?" Lift their eyes to see what could be tomorrow, not just what is today. Then lay out your plan for a new and improved initiative. People cling to what they know, but they are drawn to vision. I have found that pastors make two mistakes when it comes to leading through change. Some pastors make change too quickly. They assess the need, cast the vision, and demand rapid change. This usually results in major pushback from the stakeholders in the church who liked things the way they were just fine. Other pastors make changes too slowly. The old guard that protects the status quo intimidates them and so they never really get around to changing anything. This keeps the peace, but the church dies a slow death in the process. I have found that if you have a system in place for ongoing planning, goal setting, and evaluation, you are able to surface the changes that need to be made and move people through the process at a pace that the church can keep up with.

## COMMUNICATE, COMMUNICATE, COMMUNICATE

At every step along the way, you will be forced to communicate your plans for the future. I heard a person say one time, "The most common mistake in communication is the assumption that it has taken place." Just because you say something doesn't necessarily mean people hear you. And just because you say something once, doesn't mean people got it and are on board with you. As you communicate the vision and direction of your church, it is critical that you communicate to various people in various ways using various methods. Over the past twenty years of ministry, I've practiced what I call "Cascading Communication" when setting direction for the church. Picture a multi-level waterfall. The water flows from up top and falls to one level, then it spills from there down to another level, then spills again to another level. This continues until the water finally reaches the pool of water at the bottom of the falls. Just as water cascades down from one level to the next, communication must flow down from you to the church through various levels of leadership. If your communication hits every level of leadership in the proper order, there is cohesiveness and clarity at the bottom. However, if you skip certain levels of leadership then there is opportunity for confusion and dissension. So, what are these levels of leadership? Cascading communication starts with you. You must have absolute clarity in your mind of the direction you are headed. If something is a bit misty in your mind, it will be a total fog to the people around you. I often spend time with the Lord asking Him for clear direction and promises out of his Word to guide me. I don't want to make a mistake or lead the church in the wrong direction. I will also bounce my thoughts off of a few trusted, godly advisors who know my heart and share my passion for disciple making. On occasion I will sit down with "tribal chiefs," those influencers in the church that people respect and follow. Getting their buy-in early is critical to the success of your plans. So, level one starts with you. The second level is your leadership team. For some, this would be your church staff. For others, this would be your high-capacity volunteer team that works along side you. You want to engage your team in communication. If you have involved your team in planning, goal setting, and evaluation, then you will have brought your team to consensus. However, if you fail to engage your team, you may not have their complete buy-in at this critical level. It is very important that you work diligently to have wholesale buy-in with your leadership team before moving forward. If you don't, there is little chance your plans will succeed. The third level would be larger groups of leaders. This may be a leadership council, committees, elders, or deacons. Usually this group has been set aside by the church in some official capacity to give oversight or direction. If you have groups like that, then they need to be brought into the discussion. So far, you have been communicating with small groups. In these settings you can go into great detail about your plans, goals, and assessments. You can answer questions, respond to concerns, cast vision, and ask for input. Once you have consensus, then you move to the next level, which are volunteers of certain ministry areas. For example, you may want to communicate to all your small group leaders, or all your volunteer coordinators in a certain department. Typically, these are larger groups of people. The next level represents all volunteers. You may have a volunteer banquet or training where you take time to cast the vision to this group. As the groups get larger, your communication style begins to change. You are no longer asking for input or dialogue. Now you are setting direction and casting vision with the consensus of church leadership behind you. Ultimately, the last level is the pool of people in the church at large. This may be a vision-casting sermon or articles you release in your church's newsletter or videos you post on your website. It may involve question-and-answer sessions for church members to attend. By the time you reach the church as a whole, you have already secured the support of your upper level leaders and volunteers. At this point they have heard the vision multiple times and you have developed consensus along the way. Once the church sees that everyone is in agreement, they are more accepting of the vision you are casting. Again, this communication process takes time. Leaders who rush the process or skip certain stakeholders along the way will pay for it in the end. They might get the change quicker, but they will lack the consensus and the unity that comes with patient, deliberate communication.

Moving from tradition to evaluation is a difficult step. It is also a step that is often resisted from the leadership itself. The most common mistake leaders make here is simply not doing it. Failing to plan, failing to measure progress, failing to evaluate, failing to navigate change, and failing to communicate is simply failing to lead. Failing to lead means failing to accomplish the mission

Jesus placed in our hands. My prayer for you is that as you move through this process, the Lord himself will give you great wisdom to know what to do and great courage to do it.

People in **churches** are **like people** on planes, they don't like **sudden moves**.

Jesus **envisioned** a church **committed** to **multiplying** and taking the **gospel** to the **ends of the earth**.

# MOVE FROM ADDITION TO MULTIPLICATION

Everest is the tallest mountain in the world, towering on top of the world at 29,029 feet. Over the years, it has captured the imagination and claimed the lives of many great climbers. Its beauty and mystique draw dreamers and adventurers every year. But no one simply charges to the top of this great mountain all at one time. It requires progressing through several base camps. Each camp carries its own challenges and rewards. To reach the summit you must first reach each base camp. The first stop, simply called "base camp," sits at 17,700 feet. That's approximately three hundred feet higher than any peaks we have in the continental United States. At base camp, you can hear satellite phones buzzing, journalists and explorers exchanging stories, and it is your first exposure to freezing temperatures. Just about everything freezes at this altitude—water, damp clothes, and even toothpaste. There is an excitement in the air and a feeling of anticipation as weather reports pour in and there is talk of possible avalanches. Some climbers will realize their dream of standing on the summit. Others will have to turn back, and some won't make it home at all. The next stop is the Icefall (18,000-20,000 feet). This place is filled with hazards. Deep crevasses yawn underneath your feet. Ice pinnacles dangle overhead. The entire area groans as if it could collapse at any moment. That is why most climbers just focus on getting out of there as quickly as possible. To make it through the falls you need to get there about 4:00 a.m.—any later and the ice could start melting and avalanches are possible. The next stop is Camp 1: The Valley of Silence (20,000-21,000 feet). This is a flat, deserted area covered with a blanket of deep snow. On the outside it is beautiful, but its beauty only masks the real dangers that lie underneath. The snow covers massive crevasses that open throughout the day. Pounding headaches and tired muscles test your body and endurance. As you move through the valley, you are tied to your teammates with ropes. Staying together is critical to survival. Next is Camp 2: Rocky Patch (21,000 feet). This place is "other worldly." Clouds roll up from the lower ranges giving you a surreal feeling. Enjoy this place, because it will be the last time you will get a decent meal. Then there comes the Lhotse Wall (22,300–

26,300 feet). This ice wall stands about 4,000 feet high—beautiful, but deadly. In order to climb this wall, you must use your technical climbing skills and the right equipment. Ropes, carabineers, and crampons are standard gear. The altitude begins to play tricks on your mind, slowing your response time and fogging your thoughts, so it is important to concentrate on your every move. Then comes the Deathzone (26,000 feet). This camp sits on a plateau on the edge of the earth's atmosphere. The sky is strangely dark blue. Space is within reach. At this point, the desire for success is gone; nothing matters but survival and oxygen. Everyone feels restless and weak. It is called the Deathzone because no life can survive long at this altitude. You grab a few hours of sleep and fluids and ready yourself for the summit. Finally, the hour comes. At 11:00 p.m. you strap on your gear and head out into the night. In the distance you see a string of lights. It is the headlamps of climbers slowly moving upward to the top. It is completely silent. No one talks. Everyone is pushing their bodies to the limit, anticipating the view on the summit at the first break of dawn. You reach the south summit and around the corner is the zenith of Everest. Congratulations! You have reached the top of the world![15]

## JESUS ON THE MOUNTAIN

Jesus gathered his disciples standing on the peak of another summit. From that vantage point he could see the nations sprawled out before him. There on that peak he

---

15    *The Route-climber's Guide to Everest*, mounteverest.net.

gave his disciples a compelling vision—*"Make disciples of all nations"* (Matthew 28.18-20). On that day, Jesus envisioned a church that would take the gospel to every nation and make disciples who would make disciples. He envisioned a church committed to multiplying and taking the gospel to the ends of the earth! Jesus' vision was crystal clear and his vision hasn't changed! His vision is our vision—to create a movement of multiplication. In many respects this is our Mount Everest, our summit. We dream of the day when God uses our churches to ignite movements that transform people into thriving followers of Jesus. We dream of a day when we see men and women walk with God, reach their world, and invest in a few. We dream of a day when the influence of every church stretches across each city, each state, and around the world! That is what we go to bed dreaming about and get up thinking about—how we can play a part in the greatest cause known to man—Jesus' disciple-making movement! Just like Mount Everest, this summit is magnetic, inspiring, worth living for, and worth dying for—but at times it also appears distant, removed, and unobtainable. It's tempting to think, "God could never use me to ignite a movement like this!" Just like Everest, climbing the summit of a disciple-making vision requires progressing through several "base camps," each demanding their own sense of effort, prayer, sacrifice, and commitment. Be assured, each base camp is necessary. There are no short cuts. Failure to reach each base camp means failure to reach the summit.

## BASE CAMP 1: FOCUS

This is where the disciple-making journey begins. Here, in this place, is where would-be leaders are exposed to the vision of Jesus to ignite a disciple-making movement. The focus here is on Jesus himself: Who he is...what he has done...what it means to be a disciple of Jesus Christ... and how Jesus made disciples who changed the world. Jesus started at this base camp when he invited a few men to "come and see" (John 1.38). His invitation was to come and discover who he was and where he was headed. The focus quickly became all about Jesus. At this base camp you begin to examine the scriptures, read the Harmony of the Gospels, and discover that Jesus had an intentional plan for making disciples. You begin to wrestle with a definition of a disciple. You become convinced that Jesus' way of making disciples is THE way to make disciples. The first three steps in this book outline how to fully move through this first base camp. This step is critical if you want to fulfill Jesus' plan for your church. It is usually at this point that people either decide to move toward the summit or they follow other false summits that promise quick church growth, but don't produce multiplying disciples.

## BASE CAMP 2: BUILD

At this camp, leaders start to put into action the model of Jesus. Here you establish your key definition of a disciple. You create a process of disciple making that follows Jesus' plan, and you start choosing tools you can use to invest in people's lives. You start meeting with men before work and after hours studying the Bible, training them to pray, memorizing scripture, and showing them how to walk with God. You start intentionally making lunch appointments with people far from God and praying for opportunities to share the gospel. You start investing in your staff and demonstrating how to walk with God, reach your world, and invest in a few. Soon, those you have poured into are reaching out and investing in others. A small team of disciple makers is forming. Lives are being changed one at a time. New leaders are emerging, reproduction is happening on a limited scale. The work is hard, but you are starting to see some of the fruits of your labor. Jesus invested the majority of his time in twelve men whom he trained to do what he did, talk as he talked, and walk as he walked. He built leaders who would change the world. The danger of this camp is that resistance to disciple making can become fierce. The frigid winds of opposition, the deep crevasses of time demands, the fear of change, and the extreme effort to keep moving forward, all while you are carrying the same workload, and the alluring distractions of other programs that offer a quick trip to the summit seem to be all around you. One slip and you could fall backward, or even worse, the whole team could abandon the summit altogether. It's not uncommon for some on your team to disagree with your direction and even begin to resist your leadership or refuse to follow your example. This is why being linked together with the ropes of a common philosophy of ministry and a common vision are essential. The fourth and fifth steps outlined in this book will help you navigate through this part of your journey.

## BASE CAMP 3: ESTABLISH

Now that you have made it this far, it's time to formalize some structures. Here you begin to craft mission statements and vision statements. You start to evaluate your current church programming against Jesus' four-step process. You begin to establish core values that guide you along the way and create a common language of disciple making that helps you to communicate. This camp is dangerous because it soon becomes obvious that things cannot remain the same if the summit is to be reached. Programs must change. The measurements of success must change. No longer are the metrics of buildings, budgets, and bodies the full measurement of success. Jesus' view of success is measured in obedience to the mission to make disciples who make disciples. There are pitfalls along the way. Staff and volunteers who want the status quo or are not sold out to the summit may begin to resist change. They may resist setting goals, react defensively when their ministry is evaluated, and some may even abandon the team altogether. This is why you must carefully and intentionally set times for planning and assessment. Each time you do, you are reminding them of the summit that looms ahead. And just as talking on Everest becomes increasingly difficult, at this stage you must work hard to cascade communication, saturating every level of leadership so that the team is all working together. You may even create new forms of communication, new meetings, and new mediums to get your message across to the right people at the right time. All the while, you are keeping your key leaders close to you every step along the way. The fifth step outlined in this book will serve you well during this phase.

## CAMP 4: MULTIPLY

This last camp may be the most difficult of them all. In many ways, this step is like scaling the Lhotse Wall. It is formidable and intimidating. It requires skill and technique and not many are able to make it to this camp. Many have tried and failed. Others have abandoned the pursuit, claiming that it is impossible in "this day and age." This is the camp where multiplication begins to happen. And multiplication is what allows you to create a movement of multiplication.

## THE POWER OF MULTIPLICATION

Jesus took the men he had built and trained for over three years and he released them to multiply. This was the whole point of his investment. The twelve soon multiplied to seventy-two. In that moment, Jesus was filled with joy. He knew that the movement would happen, because they had reached base camp four—they were multiplying. In the Book of Acts, the early church is described as a multiplying church! In just two years they had "filled Jerusalem with their teaching" (Acts 5.28). In four and a half years the churches were multiplying rapidly (Acts

9.31). In nineteen years they had *"turned the world upside down"* (Acts 17.6). And in twenty-eight years, the gospel had spread all over the world (Colossians 1.56). Multiplication is a big deal to Jesus. Healthy things multiply! Dead things don't.

A few weeks ago, I decided to rake up the leaves and acorns in my front yard. The cold winds and temperatures had signaled my two oak trees that it was time to drop everything. In just about an hour I had amassed fifteen piles of acorns! As I was scooping these acorns into garbage bags and dragging them to the curb, I was reminded why trees have acorns. Every acorn represents an attempt to reproduce. There is something bound up in its nature that wants to be fruitful and multiply. Inside, every acorn contains the precise DNA and all that is necessary for one tree to produce another tree just like it! Churches are like trees. Bound up in every healthy church is the desire and the ability to reproduce. However, few churches ever truly multiply. If you read the gospels you will notice something that is sobering. Every time Jesus addresses a person or a people that refuse to multiply or bear fruit, his tone is stern. In Matthew 7, Jesus said, *"Every good tree bears good fruit..."* (vs17), but he adds, *"Every tree that does not bear fruit is cut down and thrown into the fire"* (vs19). It's worthless. It's only good for kindling. The same is found in Luke 13. Jesus tells a parable about a barren fig tree. The owner walks by, examining the fruit of his orchard, and he notices that this tree is not bearing fruit. He quickly orders it to be cut down. The gardener begs the master to give the tree one more year and so the Master agrees, but he warns: "If there is no fruit after a year cut it down." In another parable, the parable of the talents found in Matthew 25, Jesus tells the story of three servants who receive a certain amount of money to invest during their Master's absence. It is the one who did nothing with what was given to him that is punished. Even what he had was taken away. Again, in Mark 11.12-14, Jesus is traveling into Jerusalem during his last week on earth. He passes by a barren fig tree and he curses the tree because it did not bear fruit. You get the picture? It's a serious thing to not bear fruit. It's a serious thing to not multiply your life in others. And it is a serious thing to lead a barren church that never multiplies. One thing is clear, in Jesus' mind fruitfulness and spiritual multiplication are expected and necessary. Because without multiplication, there can be no movement.

## WHY DON'T CHURCHES MULTIPLY?

If Jesus is so concerned about multiplication, then why are so many pastors not concerned about it? It is interesting to me that as much as we tend to hold up the early church as the perfect model, even they struggled with multiplication. Jesus clearly told the leaders of the early church to multiply. In Acts 1.8 Jesus said, *"You shall receive power when the Holy Spirit has come upon you and you will be my witnesses in Jerusalem and in all Judea and Samaria and to the end of the earth."* Jesus wasn't vague in his command. He told them to start where they were, in Jerusalem, and work outward into the surrounding regions and ultimately to every nation. That was Jesus' plan from the beginning. But eight chapters later, the church still is operational only in Jerusalem. It wasn't until persecution came that the believers were scattered out to make disciples and establish disciple-making churches. *"And there arose on that day a great persecution against the church of Jerusalem, and they were scattered throughout the regions of Judea and Samaria, except the apostles"* (Acts 8.1). I think there are several things that can keep a person and keep a church from multiplying.

**Lack of spiritual maturity.** Reproduction requires a level of maturity. Trees don't multiply until they are fully matured. Animals and people don't multiply until they reach a certain level of maturity, and the same is true spiritually. It takes a certain level of spiritual maturity to be able to multiply your life into the life of another person. That is why multiplication is at the end of the process and not at the beginning. Jesus didn't call his disciples and immediately send them out. He called them, walked with them, trained them, and THEN released them to multiply. Some people don't multiply themselves because they still need time to grow up and mature. Unfortunately, we have equated spiritual maturity with spiritual knowledge. If a person is saved, has been in church a while, reads their Bible, and has a good base of biblical knowledge, we will say that person is mature. But maturity isn't about how much you know, it's about how much fruit you show.

Maturity is measured in fruit. Those who are fully mature in Christ are those who seek out opportunities to pour their lives into others. Now there may be obstacles to a person growing up and maturing spiritually. If there is some sin issue in a person's life that is hindering their walk with God or some area that is stunting their spiritual maturity, then that will hinder a person from bearing fruit. On the night before Jesus' death, he was talking to his disciples about bearing fruit. He equated his disciples to the branches of a vineyard. He was the vine and his Father was the vinedresser (John 15.1-8). He said (v2), "*Every branch in me that does not bear fruit he takes away.*" Some verses translate that "he cuts off." ESV has it better, "*he takes away.*" The word is (*airo*) which means to lift up, or to take to another place. The picture here is a vine that has fallen off the trellis and is down in the mud. It can't get light, it can't get air, and so it's unfruitful. And the vinedresser comes and lifts it up, cleans it off, and attaches it back to the trellis so it can bear fruit again. The reason some Christians never bear fruit is because they are mired in sin and selfishness. What they really need is to turn back to God, experience his forgiveness, and get back to the things that really matter. The same could be said for churches. There are some churches that are just not healthy. Internal conflict, tolerance of sin within the ranks, abandoning the clear preaching of the gospel— any of these things can cause a church to be unhealthy and unable to reproduce. The first step in multiplication is spiritual health.

**Distractions.** This is another reason people and churches don't multiply. Many people are very busy with many good things, but there is no time or margin in their lives to multiply themselves in others. In the parable of the sower, it was the seed that fell among the weeds that was choked out and failed to produce fruit (Matthew 13.22). I can't tell you how many businessmen I have talked to who have said, "Craig, I really want to walk with God and make disciples, but...I'm slammed at work," or, "my kids are playing ball," or, "we've got this lakehouse we need to take care of every weekend," or, "my travel schedule is crazy," or you name it. This is a person who is willing, but unwilling at the same time. They want to make disciples, but they are unwilling to prioritize disciple making in their life. Jesus alluded to this in John 15. He said for some to really begin to bear "more fruit," God needs to prune them. Pruning means cutting away the excess distractions for optimal growth. Some pastors need to cut away good things out of their church calendar so that the most important things can have space to grow. Some pastors need to prune out their own schedules so they have time to personally invest in others. Pruning can be painful. When God is pruning away internal devotions in our heart until all we have and love is him, that's painful. When you take a step back and prune away things you love to do to make room for investing in others, that's painful. There is pain in pruning, but there is fruit in pruning as well. Whether personally or corporately, distractions keep people and churches from multiplying.

**Aversion to risk.** Some people and churches do not multiply because they are afraid of change and the unknown. It all seems too risky and unsure. I believe this is what was keeping the early church from plowing right away into Judea, Samaria, and the nations. They were under intense pressure from the religious establishment. They were unsure how their message would be accepted. After all, they had just watched Jesus be crucified. They might be next. It wasn't until the heat was turned up so high in Jerusalem and they couldn't stay that they ventured out and began to reproduce. Some people just don't reach out to a person to share the gospel because they are afraid. Some never sit down over coffee and offer to invest in a new believer because there are afraid. Some churches never plant another church because they are afraid of who will leave or afraid the new plant will fail. Some people never venture to make disciples overseas because they are afraid. Fear can hold you back from making disciples if you let it. But that is why Jesus gave us the Holy Spirit to go before us. Jesus said, "You will receive power when the Holy Spirit comes on you, THEN you will be my witnesses." The power to multiply doesn't come from us, it comes from God. And the ability to override our risk aversions and act boldly and courageously comes from the Spirit he has given to each of us.

**Unwillingness to sacrifice.** Multiplication is tough. It often takes giving without getting much in return, at least in the beginning. It takes sacrifice to invest your life or multiply your ministry. The three businessmen who taught me this principle modeled sacrifice. They were very busy, successful men. But I saw them disciple men on their lunch breaks, on their days off, after hours. I saw them get up early and go to bed late because they were committed to making disciples. Their lives continue to be an example for me. Jesus said it would be this way. In Luke 9.23, as he was preparing to release his twelve men to multiply he said, *"If anyone would come after me, let him deny himself and take up his cross daily and follow me."* Self-denial and sacrifice is required if you are to multiply yourself. Think of your own family. It's a wonderful thing to have children. They bring so much joy in our lives. But many times raising kids can require self-denial. No one wants to get up at 3:00 a.m. to change a diaper. No one wants to put kids to bed seven times because they are afraid of the dark. No one wants to spend money for braces and ball lessons. But we do. Why? Because we love them and because what little sacrifices we make are more than worth it for the joy of seeing them grow. The same is true spiritually. Yes, it takes sacrifice to invest in people. Yes, it takes time, effort, and patience. Sometimes the very people you pour your life into will disappoint you or hurt you, just as your children do at times. We do it because the joy in life and ministry is in seeing those we have led to the Lord and trained to walk with God being used in a powerful way. The Apostle John put it best: *"I have no greater joy than to hear that my (spiritual) children are walking in the truth"* (3 John 1.4). Listen, we must keep an eternal perspective. Our time on this earth is not for our comfort and convenience. That is what heaven is for. Our time here is to do the work that the Father has given us to do (John 9.4). Doing that work will often require us to say "goodbye" to some things we love for a while, so more can be with us in heaven forever. In order for your church to multiply, it may require you saying goodbye to a few church members to start a new church plant. It may require you to say "goodbye" to a hobby so you have more time to invest. But when you say "goodbye," you are able to say "hello" to the joy of multiplying your life in others.

**Lack of dependence on God.** Maybe this one is at the core of them all. When we are not living in prayerful dependence on Jesus, then we shrink back from obeying him fully in our lives. When I am fully surrendered to him and drawing my joy from him alone, then I am ready to be used in a powerful way. That last night, Jesus was driving these things in the minds of men. He had spent three plus years investing in them, training them, challenging and stretching them. Now it was time for him to leave and it was time for them to take the leadership of the movement. I think as he spoke these words he made eye contact with each one, letting the words linger in the air. *"I am the vine; you are the branches. Whoever abides in me and I in him, he it is that bears much fruit, for apart from me you can do nothing."* Those words are just as true today as you read them as they were when Jesus spoke them. Jesus calls each of us to abide in him. To make our home and our joy in him. He invites us to walk with him in a deep, personal, and intimate way. To draw close enough to hear his voice and follow his lead. To draw our significance and identity and hope and comfort from him and nothing else that this world offers us. The Christian life is all about Jesus. Those who walk with Jesus like that find that their lives produce a spiritual harvest. Jesus said that those who abide in him will bear "much fruit." In Matthew 13, he indicated that it would be a harvest some thirty, sixty, and hundred fold! Don't you want that for your life? Don't you want at the end of your life to look over your shoulder and see behind a wake of people that have come to Christ, and are walking with Christ all because you ignited a movement one person at a time? I sure do! And I know that will require me to stay close to Jesus and abide in him one day at a time.

## THREE WAYS TO MULTIPLY YOUR MINISTRY

Much of the attention of pastors has been on growing their ministry. Growing usually implies having more people attend than did the week or month before. In order to grow, new people must be added to the church. So in that sense, growth is all about addition. Adding new people. Adding new staff. Adding new programs. Adding new givers to the organization. Adding new volunteers. Adding new facilities. Now don't get me wrong, addition is not a bad thing. We need to add new people, new believers, and new leaders if we want to stay strong and healthy. Even in Acts 2.41, after Peter preached at

Pentecost ,the Spirit writes, *"...and there were added that day about three thousand souls."* Addition is a good thing. But addition should not be confused with multiplication. Multiplying your ministry requires investing in others so they are released to invest in others, thereby creating exponential growth. Let me give you four ways you can begin to multiply the ministry in your church.

***Personal multiplication.*** Personal multiplication is when a believer personally reproduces his or her life in the life of another person. This may happen when a seasoned Christ follower builds a relationship with a friend far from God and over time the gospel is shared and that person comes to faith in Jesus. That's spiritual reproduction. It may happen when a believer reaches out to another new Christian and offers to walk alongside them and show them how to walk with God, reach their world, and invest in a few. When that happens, that is spiritual reproduction. Where this gets confusing for some is when people think that leading a Bible study or a small group qualifies as spiritual multiplication. They say, "I'm helping people grow," and that is true. But this is not multiplication because there is no intentional plan for the person they have trained to then go out and train others. Our churches are filled with Bible studies, small groups, and midsized groups. But most of that ministry ends when the study is over. Multiplication happens when a person is trained to invest their life in another person so that they can do the same. That's personal multiplication.

*Group multiplication.* Group multiplication is when a group, led by disciple makers, grows to the point that they must "birth" a new group. First you had one group, now you have two. Theoretically, if those two groups birth new groups, then the two become four and hopefully the four become eight and so on. That is group multiplication. Again, the stated goal of the group is to at some point multiply. Eventually, as these groups grow in number, the church as a whole grows numerically. As cells in a body grow, divide, and multiply, so the groups in a healthy church grow, divide, and multiply. This type of multiplication is more complicated than just personal multiplication. In order for a group to multiply you must do three things. Think of them by the acrostic V.I.P. First, there must be vision. The group must have a vision to reach as many people as possible. Second, there must be invested leaders. These are leaders who have been discipled; they know how to walk with God, reach their world, and invest in a few. And third, there must be a plan to multiply. The group must have a clear, intentional, thoughtful plan of how they are going to reach people, disciple and raise up leaders, and launch a new group. Now that being said, the reason why groups don't multiply is usually because they lack those three vital elements. Many groups don't have a vision for multiplication. Their goal is to stay together as long as possible. When a group is truly experiencing community, it's hard to leave it. By nature we want to huddle together, the proverbial "us for no more" mentality. You can tell when a group has a negative view of multiplication because they will say things like, "You're not trying to split my group are you?" For these people, keeping the group together is their mission, not reaching people. As I said earlier in this chapter, multiplication requires sacrifice. Sometimes that means sacrificing an hour a week with a certain group of people so I can reach more people who don't know Jesus. I remember speaking at a church groups' training, and a couple was interviewed. They had been a part of starting over sixteen different groups in their church. Once they would get a group started and raise up leaders, they were ready to start another. Their motive was to reach as many people as possible with the time God gave them. We need more people like that in our church, and we can have them if we raise them up! Another factor that keeps groups from growing is the lack of investing in emerging leaders. Many times, group leaders like their role and don't want anything to take it away. Every new emerging teacher or leader is viewed as a threat to their coveted position. But multiplying groups are always on the lookout for new leaders that they can invest in, disciple and prepare for leadership. And ultimately, groups don't multiply if they don't have a stated plan to do so. Most groups are just meeting weekly with little thought for what their one-year or two-year plan might be. Multiplying groups start off thinking about where they are headed. They have a vision to multiply, they invest in their leaders to multiply and they have a plan to multiply.

*Church multiplication.* This last approach to multiplication happens when a church multiplies, creating other disciple-making churches. This may happen through church planting, re-planting or multi-site expansion. Ralph Moore, in his great book, *How to Multiply your Church* said that we need to *"stop counting converts and start counting congregations."*[16] Again, just like with group multiplication, there are few churches that have the vision, invested leadership, and a plan to actually multiply. Many pastors see church planting in a negative light, siphoning off much needed leadership and financial resources from the church they are leading. Replants have recently come in vogue. This is where a healthy, established church takes over a dying church and basically re-plants a new congregation in the facility of the old church. Multi-site models are also quite popular today. This is where a strong healthy church sets up multiple locations in various parts of the city and/or world. The majority of the top 100 fastest growing churches in America are multi-site churches. While the scope of this book is not able to delve into the various options for church multiplication, the disciple-making pastor must find a way to multiply their ministry to reach as many as possible.

When I pastored the church in Oklahoma City, we were in a downtown transitional neighborhood. The church had been plateaued for decades and all the churches around us were in steep decline and many were dying. The communities were extremely diverse. If you went to

---

16    *How to Multiply Your Church*, Ralph Moore page 25.

the north a few blocks from the church, the majority of the population was African American. The schools were rough and the tagged buildings made it clear that gangs were a fact of everyday life. If you went to the east about two blocks, you were in little Vietnam. All the store and business advertisements were in Vietnamese. People spoke that language fluently and even the doctor's offices and grocery stores were dominated by the culture. Also in this part of town sat Oklahoma City University, a school that boasted of a huge international student population. If you went two blocks south of the church you were in little Mexico. A huge Mexican market covered a city block. Spanish was the dominant language and for not much money you could find some amazing Mexican food restaurants. If you went west of the church, across the highway, you would find several Anglo neighborhoods, mostly smaller, middle-class homes that were either owned by retirees or being bought and remodeled by younger couples. It was the most diverse place I had ever experienced. The majority of the people who attended the church didn't even live in these neighborhoods. Most lived in a circle around the church five to ten miles out in the suburbs and drove in on the weekends. How would we ever reach a diverse community, much less help our people reach those they know in the suburbs? Our strategy was simple: multiply. We began by launching new congregations in our church facility to reach a people segment in our community. Over the course of several years we birthed four new churches, reaching four new language-based people groups: Vietnamese, Korean, Spanish, and International. Later, the churches branched out even further to reaching other people groups as well. All of these churches started out in the church chapel that seated comfortably about one hundred people. One of the new church pastors named the chapel the "womb of the church" because we had birthed so many new churches from there. One of my favorite memories of that church was Thanksgiving weekend. Every year on this Sunday, all the congregations would gather together for one joined service. I can remember it like it was yesterday. As the worship music played, each new congregation would parade into the auditorium to the applause of the whole body. It felt like opening night at the Olympics. During the service each group would lead out in some element of worship. The Korean band would sing in their language, the Spanish church leaders would read scripture, Vietnamese children would dance in their cultural dress. Then we would all take Communion together. As I read a passage of scripture, each pastor would translate it into their unique language. Then we would all sing the final song together, but in our own language. Somehow we knew that what sounded confusing on earth sounded beautiful in heaven! But that is not all. We not only focused on planting congregations in the inner-city, but we also planted new locations in the suburbs. We launched the first multi-site church in the state of Oklahoma in a convention center building northwest of town. I would preach the early service at the North campus, then get in my car and drive downtown to the Central campus for worship. I'll never forget casting vision and seeing the people jump at the chance to serve. While the whole "multi-site strategy" was extremely new, they were eager to reach people who lived close to them. At the same time, we launched new groups designed to reach inner-city kids in the public schools. We forged alliances with the six schools in our area and provided them with supplies, clothing and tutors. We hosted speakers in the schools that brought an anti-drug message and then shared the gospel. We hosted an annual breakfast for all the teachers and administrators to encourage them and pray for them. During this time the principal that ran the middle school across the street had a son lying in the hospital dying of cancer. He was a bright young man, only nineteen years old. When I went to visit him, I talked to him about Jesus and about how he could know for sure he would be in heaven. He took my hand and said, "I want to know Jesus." A few weeks later, our church was filled with teachers, coaches, and administrators as I preached his funeral. The entire community had embraced us as their church because we had embraced us with the love of Christ. That spring, the Oklahoma City Independent School District hosted a gala at the downtown Cox Convention Center. It was a formal event broadcast across the whole city on television. During the program, they recognized three community partners that had made a difference in students' lives. Those three partners were Chesapeake Energy, The Daily Oklahoman, and our church. As I stood to receive our award, they played a video of our people at work loving on kids and teachers. I saw clips of our members painting walls, cleaning bathrooms, tutoring students, feeding and hugging teachers all to the sound of thunderous applause and a standing ovation. I couldn't help but think that all of heaven was celebrating, too! The words flashed in my mind, "Let your light shine before others, so that they may see your good works and give glory to your Father who is in heaven" (Matthew 5.16). When you set your heart to multiply your church, people will notice and God will get the glory.

During that season of ministry, we saw the church grow numerically and baptize more that it had in years. It was a very fruitful season because we were committed to multiplication. Was it difficult doing all the work that went into starting new churches, launching another site, serving the community, and planting churches overseas? Was it difficult investing in leaders and discipling people to walk like Jesus? Was it a struggle doing all that in an inner city church that was so limited in resources? The short answer is yes. But was it worth it? Absolutely. You can do this, too. No matter the size or budget of your church, you can commit yourself to multiplication. You can begin to invest in emerging leaders personally and train them how to walk with God, reach their world and invest in a few. You can then place those new disciple makers in key roles to launch new groups. Those groups then become places where they reach new people and disciple them. As your groups mature, you infuse them with vision, invested leadership, and a plan to multiply. Then release those groups to reach their community with the gospel. Eventually, missional groups reaching their communities become the core of a new church plant, replant, or ministry site. Nothing is impossible with God. He wants to use you and your church to do things you never dreamed possible. And he will do it through you as you trust him and follow his lead.

# The **power** to **multiply** doesn't come from us, it comes **from God**.

**If** you are
going to **make
disciples**, **now**
is the **time** to
be busy.

# URGENCY OF THE HOUR

It was late in Jesus' ministry. Already he had invested over three years of his life into a group of men who he believed would carry on the movement he had begun. The future looked promising. Just a few months earlier, Jesus told his disciples in Caesarea Philippi, *"If anyone would come after me, let him deny himself and take up his cross daily and follow me" (Luke 9.23).* From that moment, Jesus set his face toward Jerusalem, committed to do there what he had come to earth to do. And his men faithfully followed him. Soon they began to multiply. The twelve turned into seventy-two and they scattered throughout the villages and towns preaching the gospel and pointing people to Jesus (Luke 10.1). All the while, the pressure from the religious leaders increased exponentially. Clandestine plots to capture Jesus and insidious strategies to take his life were already underway. Jesus knew the time to embrace the cross was drawing closer. Every moment counted. No time could be wasted. What he did in these final days mattered. There was a sense of urgency, focus and determination written on his face. Around this time Jesus and his disciples approached a man born blind, sitting in the temple. An unnamed disciple posed Jesus the question, "Who sinned," pointing to the man, "this man or his parents that he was born blind?" In other words, "What did he do wrong for God to allow this to come upon him?" Jesus stopped for a teaching moment and replied, *"It was not that this man sinned or his parents, but that the works of God might be displayed in him"* (John 9.3). This tragedy was not a result of sin, and it wasn't a punishment from God; rather, it was a platform God would use to exalt himself through this man's life. Then Jesus added these words, *"We must work the works of him who sent me while it is still day, night is coming when no one can work"* (John 9.4). Every time I read those words I can feel the sense of urgency in Jesus. I can see him lock eyes with his men, capturing their attention, as if he was about to make a statement that he never wanted them to forget. "Men, never forget this. Just as God wants to use this man's infirmity to bring glory to himself, in the same way God wants to use you to bring him glory. That's why we must give ourselves fully to this work he has given us to do, because our time is short. What we are going to do, we must do now." I believe that now, more than ever, Jesus is calling out leaders who will join him in this great work.

As I have reflected on this passage over the years, some things stand out that keep me motivated and driven to make disciples for the rest of my life.

## THE WORK IS DISCIPLE MAKING

Jesus put it plainly, "*We must work the works of him who sent me*" (John 9.4). The work Jesus was talking about was making disciples that would produce disciple makers. This is the work he has left us to do. Flash back to the first year in Jesus' ministry. He was standing alone by a well in Samaria. His disciples had just returned from the market to grab some lunch for Jesus. Little did they know that Jesus had just finished a powerful conversation with a woman at the well that would set in motion an entire community coming to know and to follow Christ. As they insisted that he eat, Jesus replied, "*My food is to do the will of him who sent me and to accomplish his work*" (John 4.34). It was as if Jesus was saying to them, "Guys, there is nothing more satisfying and fulfilling than doing the work my Father has sent me here to do!" What was the work he was doing? It was drawing people to him and raising up disciples. Listen, there is nothing more satisfying in ministry than making disciples. Record attendances come and go. Large events come and go. Building projects and mission trips come and go. But the one thing that will satisfy you in ministry is pouring your life into a few people and watching them do the same thing. That never gets old. That is where the joy in ministry is found. Now, flash forward to the last night of Jesus. He is sitting with his disciples, sharing a Passover meal. His heart is full as he lifts his eyes toward heaven to pray. *"I glorified you here on the earth having accomplished the work that you gave me to do"* (John 17.4). Let me ask you a question. What was the "work" Jesus was referring to here? It certainly wasn't the work of going to the cross. That had not happened yet. Jesus said that he had accomplished this work. The word "accomplished" is the same root word that Jesus spoke on the cross when he said *"It is finished"* (John 19.30). What work had Jesus finished that glorified the Father? What work had the Father given him to do? It was the work of making disciples who would reproduce. Pastor, this is the same work Jesus has placed in your hands and in mine. Jesus never put in our hands the work of building a large church or preaching great sermons. He put in our hands the work of making disciples who would carry the gospel and multiply.

## THE PARTNERSHIP IS WITH JESUS

I find a great deal of comfort in Jesus' words here. *"We must work the works of him who sent me."* The "we" jumps off the page at me. It is an amazing thing to think that as you are making disciples, you are actually in partnership with Jesus. There is no time that you are walking more closely in Jesus' steps than when you are following his example by investing your life in others. There is never a time when you are more reflecting the heart and passion of Jesus than when you are pouring your life into another person. There is a supernatural fellowship with Jesus that you experience in the trenches of disciple making that isn't experienced anywhere else. I believe this is why Jesus gave that wonderful promise at the end of his disciple-making commission. He had just said, "Go make disciples of all nations," then he adds, "and I will be with you." I can tell you that when I meet with men early in the mornings and I pour my life into them, I feel the presence of Jesus in a powerful way. I feel his pleasure. I can sense him saying, "Craig, this is what it's all about! Invest your life, just like I invested mine."

There is a church southeast of Rome that sits along the ancient highway called the Appian Way. It has been a sacred place for centuries, however, the church was built in 1637. The church is called "Domine Quo Vadis," which means "Lord, where are you going?" According to the apocryphal Acts of Peter, a legend is told that Peter was in Rome during the outbreak of persecution against the Christians at the hand of Caesar Nero. Under the cover of night, Peter escaped Rome and was traveling down the Appian Way when he had a vision of Jesus walking toward him. Bewildered, Peter asked him, "*Domine, quo vadis?*"—"Lord where are you going?" To which Jesus replied, "*Eo Romam iterum crucifigi.*"—"I am going to Rome to be crucified again." Ashamed, Peter returned back to Rome, and there he was eventually captured and crucified upside down for his faith. This encounter is depicted in Annibale Carracci's 1602 painting, "Peter's Meeting with Christ." If you were to ask Jesus today, "Lord, where are you going? Where are you leading? How do you want me to walk as you have walked?" I believe his answer would be clear. "Go make disciples of all nations." The real question is, "Are you following?" Are you willing to give yourself to this great cause of disciple making, or are you headed in a different direction? I'm so glad that I turned around and followed Jesus into this life of investing in others. I have been forever changed.

# THE URGENCY OF THE HOUR

Jesus' words have an urgency about them. The New Living Translation picks up on it. *"We must quickly carry out the tasks assigned us by the one who sent us. The night is coming, and then no one can work"* (John 9.4, NLT). We must quickly be about this business. Why? Because night is coming, soon no man can work. I grew up in West Texas in a small community surrounded by farm land. I can still remember the farmers working until all hours of the night stripping the cotton, and hauling massive white bundles to the local gin for processing. At times, stray fragments of cotton would cover the roads like a mild winter snow. Before electricity, there was a real sense of urgency to get the crop in once it was ready to be harvested. Men would work long and hard in the fields, but they had to work quickly because night was coming when all work had to stop. That is what Jesus had in mind here. We are laboring in the field—reaching people for Christ and walking with them to maturity. It takes work and sustained effort. It takes vision and determination. It takes the patience and endurance of a farmer. But there will come a time when we can no longer do it. Night is coming when all work will stop. That coming night may be the Lord's return. When he comes, all the redemptive work of sharing the gospel and making disciples will be over. The harvest will be in. The coming night may be the end of your life. Your days are numbered. Your time is short. The days for you to invite people to know Jesus and invest in people to walk like Jesus are coming to a close. No matter which one Jesus had in mind, his call is urgent. We don't have all the time in the world. If you are going to make disciples, now is the time to be busy. Now is the time to invest your life. Now is the time to lead like you have never led before, because night is coming when your work will be done.

Jesus' call is an urgent call to action. And action is needed because so much is a stake. Think about it. The church is at stake. How much longer do you really think the church will be able to sustain itself if disciple making is ignored? Already we are seeing the signs of decline, but Jesus gave us the simple solution. Make disciples. When you look at history, revival, and spiritual awakenings have gone hand in hand with disciple making—from the great awakenings of Europe to the Jesus movement in the 1970s. The church in America today desperately needs to turn back to making disciples. The lives of those far from God are at stake. How will this world be reached? How will the nations hear the gospel? They will hear it from men and women who are sold out to Jesus and know how to multiply their lives in others. They will hear from men and women who have decided to take up their crosses and follow Jesus. The hearts of the people in your church are at stake. Right now, there are people in your church who desperately need someone to show them how to walk with God. They need someone to come alongside them, show them how to walk with God, how to reach their world, and invest in a few. How will they grow if you do not show them? How will they mature if you do not provide someone to pour into their lives? The impact of your ministry is at stake. Robert Coleman, in his book, *The Master Plan of Evangelism*, makes a poignant statement. *"One must decide where he wants his ministry to count—in the momentary applause of popular recognition or in the reproduction of his life in a few chosen ones who will carry on his work after he has gone? Really, it is a question of which generation we are living for."*[17] Where do you want your life to count? Will your ministry be something that achieved a certain level of temporary success, only to be forgotten after you are gone? Will the sermons you preach and the buildings you build become objects of the past with little lasting value? Surely God wants your ministry to be more than that! If you invest your life in others and teach them to do the same, your ministry will always be reaching the next generation. Your ministry will always bear lasting fruit, fruit that remains until Jesus comes, and you will prove yourself to be a true disciple of Jesus (John 15.8). Don't buy into the lure of temporary success. Invest your life for the long haul. Your

17    Robert Coleman, *The Master Plan of Evangelism*, page 37.

life can be more than just managing a church…it can be about joining a movement that changes the world. Don't settle for anything less.

When I think about these things, I picture myself throwing a rock into a pristine lake. The water is glass. There is a stillness in the air. I draw back and release the stone with all the force I can muster. I see it tumble in the air, drawing an arc in the sky, until it plummets to the water's surface. Splash! Immediately, the rock vanishes underneath. In many ways your life is like that. You are a stone in flight, making a splash on this Earth. But no matter how big a splash you make, it is only for a moment, and then you will disappear from here. Soon the lake will return back as it was before. But if you give yourself to making disciples and you teach them to do the same, you can leave behind ripples of multiplication. Life on life, flowing from one to the other, until the movements reach the banks of the shore. Your one life can ignite a movement that continues until Jesus returns. So, let's give ourselves to this call of Jesus. Let's make the bold moves. Let's throw our lives into making disciples like Jesus so that when he comes he will find that our lives were fruitful and that his glory was put on display!

It is **not** about **how much** you know; it's about **how you live**..

# APPENDIX

Over the years, as I have talked with many leaders about how to lead their churches to become disciple-making churches, a simple graph has proven helpful in understanding the four key phases of Jesus' ministry. As I mentioned in chapter three, Jesus had a clear process for making reproducing disciples. That process was simply to move men through four phases of spiritual development. The end product was a reproducing disciple who looked like Jesus and carried on the mission of Jesus to the ends of the earth. Before you look over this visual summary, let me make a few clarifying statements.

First, this diagram is descriptive. Each phase represents a stage in a person's spiritual development. Every person in your church (or anyone alive for that matter) falls into one of these four phases. This can be extremely useful when helping a person identify where they are spiritually and their next step. Recently, I took an executive to lunch and he was describing his desire to grow spiritually. I took a napkin and drew out this simple diagram, explaining each phase and sharing that Jesus took his men through each step. I could already see the wheels turning in his mind. He was self-assessing based on this simple tool. The descriptive nature of this tool is also helpful for leaders as they identify where a person is spiritually. Often people will self-assess much further along in the process than they really are because they have been in church a while or they have accumulated quite of bit of spiritual knowledge. But this graph is not about how much you know; it's about how you live. Leaders need some kind of objective benchmark to know how to help their people identify and take the next step in their spiritual growth.

Second, this diagram is successive. Jesus moved people through these phases in a successive order. Starting left and moving right, he moved his men through each phase, from the explore phase to the connect phase to the grow phase and ultimately to the multiply phase. Some people like to think they can skip around and achieve the same results. Now, back to the executive in the restaurant. After some reflection he realized that he wanted to be in the grow phase, but he had skipped over the connect phase. He then proceeded to tell me why he didn't need that phase and how it would not benefit him. I just kept eating my lunch and listening carefully. Then I asked him, "What would you tell one of your employees if they said they wanted to circumvent a key portion of your training process because they didn't think they needed it?" Again the wheels were turning in his mind. I continued, "You see, Jesus knows what he is doing. This isn't my program, it's his program and each phase is critical to the end product. Skip a stage, and the end result isn't the same." He nodded in agreement. Identifying these stages helps a person to know the next step on their journey. Honestly, most people don't think there is a next step for them. They think that once they are saved and baptized, the rest of their life is destined to be spent sitting in a group or handing out programs at the worship center door. When they realize that there is a next step before them, they become energized and excited.

Third, this diagram is progressive. To move from one step to the next requires progressively greater commitment and greater sacrifice. It takes some effort to explore the claims of Christ, but it takes even greater commitment to cross the faith line by repenting and believing in Jesus. It takes even more commitment to be baptized and connect to a church, even more to join a group, even more to serve, even more to be trained as a disciple, and even more to multiply your life. With each step greater commitment, greater sacrifice and greater resolve is required. You will notice on the diagram a diagonal line. Below the line represents the commitment level required at each phase. You will notice that the commitment rises as you progress through each phase.

There is not much commitment at all in the explore phase, but there is great commitment and sacrifice required at the multiplication phase. The line also represents the number of people willing to move to the next grow phase. If you look at everything above the diagonal line, you notice that as you go through the phases the number of people willing to make that commitment and follow Jesus gets smaller and smaller. This was certainly the case in Jesus' ministry. Thousands of people gathered to hear him speak and watch him perform miracles. Fewer were willing to truly follow him and join his new community of believers. Even fewer were trained as leaders. Initially, only a handful were proven multipliers. But it was through those few that the movement began and the church reproduced rapidly. This diagram is important for leaders because it is a reminder that not everyone is going to go with you through each phase. Not everyone followed Jesus, and not everyone will follow you. However, for those who do, those who are the few who multiply their lives, they become the tip of the spear for your ministry. They are the ones who are walking with God, reaching their world, investing in a few and leading the ministry. Those are the men and women of your ministry who will multiply it long after you are gone.

Jesus was the Master at moving people through each phase. He didn't force people to take their next step. He didn't guilt them. He moved people through each phase by invitation and celebration. He would invite people to the next phase. "Come and see." "Follow me." "Be with me." "Come after me." Each of those statements were invitations to the next stage of spiritual growth. Some took him up on his invitation, but some walked away. Jesus also celebrated when a person took a faith step. Jesus said all of heaven celebrates when one person repents (Luke 15.7,10). For the leader, these phases give him something to invite his people toward, and are key celebration points along the way. As I mentioned in chapter six, it provides a rubric for you to assess the primary purpose of each ministry program and a way to assess if your ministry offering is balanced and moving people toward the end product of a healthy, reproducing disciple of Jesus.

[See diagram on next page]

Number of people moving
through each phase

Crossing
the finish line

# EXPLORE
# CONNE

**Key phrase**

"Come and see"

"Follow me

**Approximate
time Jesus
spent in
each phase**

18 months*

6 months

SALVATION

Connect peop
- Christ through

- Church through
  membership &
  baptism

**Purpose of
the phase**

Help people
explore the claims
of Christ and find
answers to their
spiritual questions.

- Community thro
  group life

- Cause through

**Key scripture**

John 1:39

Matthew 4:18

\* For more information on the time Jesus spent in each phase see
"A Harmony of the Gospels" by Thomas and Gundry, Harper & Row, Publishe

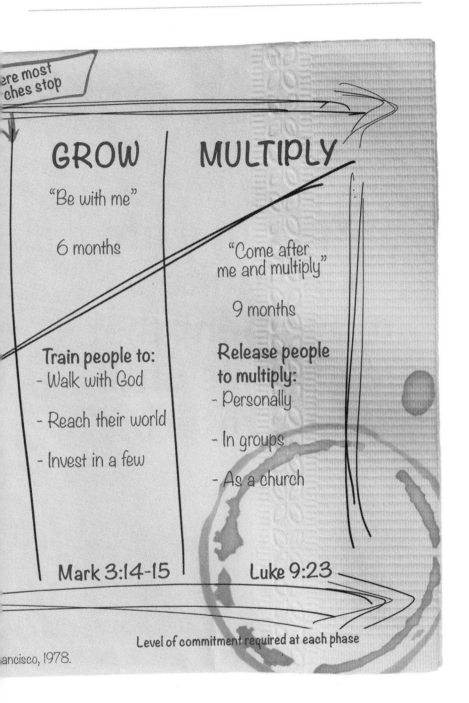

ere most
ches stop

## GROW

"Be with me"

6 months

**Train people to:**
- Walk with God
- Reach their world
- Invest in a few

Mark 3:14-15

## MULTIPLY

"Come after
me and multiply"

9 months

**Release people
to multiply:**
- Personally
- In groups
- As a church

Luke 9:23

Level of commitment required at each phase

ancisco, 1978.

# **Your** one **life** **can ignite** a **movement** that continues **until** **Jesus returns**.

# ENDNOTES

## Chapter One

Krejcir R. J. Ph.D. (n..d.). Statistics and reasons for church decline. Church leadership.org *Francis A. Schaeffer Institute of Church Leadership Development.*

## Chapter Two

Gerhard Kittle, *Theological Dictionary of the New Testament* (Grand Rapids, Michigan: Eerdmans Publishing Company, 1964), page 210.

*Robert Coleman, The Master Plan of Evangelism (Grand Rapids, Michigan: Fleming H. Revell), page 24.*

*Bill Hull, Jesus Christ Disciple Maker (Old Tappan, New Jersey: Fleming H. Revell Company, 1984), page 81.*

Shattuck, Kelly. (n.d.). Seven startling facts: an up close look at church attendance in America. Churchleaders.com.

### Chapter Three

Foster, Robert. (n.d.). Discipleship in the New Testament. Society of Biblical Literature sbl-site.org.

"New research on the state of discipleship", Barna.org.

Carl Wilson, With Christ is the school of Disciple Building (Fayetteville, Georgia, Worshipwide discipleship Association books, 1976), pg 219.

Michael J. Wilkins, Following the Master (Grand Rapids, Michigan: Zondervan Publishing House, 1992), pages 105-106.

### Chapter Five

LeRoy Eims, The Lost Art of Disciple Making (Grand Rapids, Michigan: Zondervan, 1978), page 61.

George Gallup Jr, "Why are women more religious", Gallup.com, December 17, 2002.

"Quick facts on the gender gap", Churchformen.com.

### Chapter Six

Paul Vittelo, "Taking a Break from the Lord's Work", New York Times, August 1, 2010.

Steve Addison, Movements that change the world (Downers Grove, Il: Intervarsity Press, 2009), page 29.

### Chapter Seven

Much of the information on Everest was retrieved from: "The Route-Climbers Guide to Everest", mounteverest.net

Ralph Moore, How to multiply your church (Grand Rapids, Michigan: Baker Publishing Group, 2009)," page 25.

### Chapter Eight

Robert Coleman, The Master Plan of Evangelism (Grand Rapids, Michigan: Fleming H. Revell), page 37.

## About FlashPoint Disciple-Making Conferences

1. Cast a vision of WHAT disciple making is, WHO the model is we should follow, and HOW we can implement disciple-making principles both corporately and personal life.

2. Equip attendees with a solid foundation of disciple-making principles and best practices to implement in their area of ministry and personal life. These principles and best practices are from a variety of resources and will give each attendee a broad spectrum of information.

3. Provide tools and resources, with excellence, to assist attendees in the implementation of a disciple-making movement.

# www.FlashPointConference.com

# disciple**FIRST**

**For other resources and materials from
Craig Etheredge please visit:
www.discipleFirst.com.**